THE JEWISH QUARTERLY

The Jewish Quarterly is published four times a year
by The Jewish Quarterly Pty Ltd
Publisher: Morry Schwartz

ISBN 9781922517081 E-ISBN 9781743822661
ISSN 0449010X E-ISSN 23262516

Subscriptions 1 year print & digital (4 issues): $74.99 AUD | £42 GBP |
$56 USD. 1 year digital only: $44.99 AUD | £25 GBP | $32 USD. Payment may
be made by Mastercard or Visa. Payment includes postage and handling.

To subscribe, fill out the form in this issue, subscribe online at
jewishquarterly.com, email subscribe@jewishquarterly.com or call 1800 077 514 /
+61 3 9486 0288. Correspondence should be addressed to: The Editor, The
Jewish Quarterly, 22–24 Northumberland Street, Collingwood VIC 3066
Australia
Phone +61 3 9486 0288 Email enquiries@jewishquarterly.com

The Jewish Quarterly is published under licence from the
Jewish Literary Trust Limited, which exercises a governance function.

UK Company Number: 01189861. UK Charity Commission Number: 268589.

Issue 249, August 2022

THE JEWISH QUARTERLY

Contributors

Arie M. Dubnov is an associate professor and Max Ticktin Chair of Israel Studies at the George Washington University. His books include an intellectual biography of Isaiah Berlin and two edited volumes, *Zionism* and *Partitions*.

Kim Ghattas is a contributing writer for *The Atlantic*, a senior non-resident fellow at the Carnegie Endowment for International Peace and the author of *Black Wave*.

Mark Glanville is a writer and classical singer. His work includes the memoir *The Goldberg Variations* and the forthcoming album *Citizens of Nowhere: Songs by Mieczylaw Weinberg*.

William F.S. Miles is a professor of political science at Northeastern University in Boston and author of *Paradox in Paradise*. His travel essays have appeared in many publications, including *The Boston Globe*.

Ryan Ruby is the author of *The Zero and the One: A Novel*. His criticism has appeared in *The New York Times*, *The Nation* and *New Left Review*. He lives in Berlin.

Sarah Abrevaya Stein is Viterbi Family Chair in Mediterranean Jewish Studies at UCLA. Her most recent book is *Family Papers: A Sephardic Journey Through the Twentieth Century*.

Iran

Inside its 43-year quest to
dominate the Middle East

Kim Ghattas

In 1977, in a televised interview, former US president Richard Nixon described how the leader of the Soviet Union, Leonid I. Brezhnev, was seeking world domination, following a dictum by Vladimir Lenin: "Probe with bayonets. If you find mush, proceed. If you find steel, withdraw."

"That's the way Communist leaders will be all over the world," Nixon said at the time, explaining Lenin's thinking about waging a war of indirect aggression. "That's what they believe. They want not just a Communist Russia, or what have you; they want a Communist world." Lenin's words became popular with political scientists and American foreign policymakers, who called for steely resolve in the face of the Soviet Union. Communism did not take over the world and the Soviet Union collapsed in 1991, yet Lenin's words are still being used to call for steadfast determination in the face of today's Russia and its president, Vladimir Putin – or to criticise those who show mush.

But Lenin's adage resonates well beyond the US–Russia arena in ways that seem to escape American foreign policymakers. Nixon repeated the maxim in his autobiography, published in May

1978 – just as the Iranian revolution was in full swing. Barely a year later, the Shah went into exile and in his place rose a taciturn, authoritarian, dogmatic radical who hijacked an ostensibly secular leftist revolutionary movement and turned Iran into an Islamic republic.

Ayatollah Ruhollah Khomeini's deep contempt and enmity for the United States was apparent early on. Latching on to widespread anti-imperial leftist sentiments of the era, he declared in a speech in 1980 that "the most important and painful problem confronting the subjugated nations of the world, both Muslim and non-Muslim, is the problem of America … America is the number-one enemy of the deprived and oppressed people of the world."

The Islamic Republic of Iran has been prodding America with a bayonet ever since, with quite some success. Although world domination is certainly not within Iran's reach, its ability to frustrate, irritate and even kill extends all the way to Berlin and Argentina. Within the Middle East, Iran does have expansionary ambitions and has made indirect confrontation with the United States a fundamental pillar of its foreign policy and a defining element of its domestic identity. This has been – and remains – the central tenet of the Iranian revolution.

Now, more than four decades after Khomeini founded the Islamic Republic, opposition to the United States is as much about ideology as it is about survival, power and ambition. The Iranian regime's survival depends on having an external enemy, and it has perfected the art of standing in opposition to the United States to maintain and solidify its grip on power. Ali Khamenei, who succeeded Khomeini as supreme leader in 1989, believes that compromising on any revolutionary principles – compulsory veiling for women, for example, or the slogan "Death to America" – could dilute the regime's power and hasten its demise, just as Mikhail Gorbachev's perestroika and glasnost brought down the Soviet Union.

But what does Iran actually want to do with that power?

The answer depends on how one views Iran. There are those who empathise with Iran's lists of grievances against the West and even its Arab neighbours; others take a hard line on Iran's expansionist policies and its declared enmity against Israel. Then there are those who listen to Iran's grievances to better understand its ambitions and devise policies to contain them, and stuck in the middle are those who live at the sharp end of Iranian power, from Baghdad to Beirut. But whether Iran is driven by grievances or pure power, the end goal is the same: cutting back US influence in the Middle East, by any means possible, and expanding its own influence in the region.

"Iran challenges the US as an end in itself; it's a core interest," Michael Singh, managing director of the Washington Institute and a former senior director at the National Security Council, told me. "Their ultimate goal is to usher the US out of the region so they can be top dog. They see the US as their only rival."

Iran's strategy is to eat away at American power, while legitimising its own role as a regional power with nuclear ambitions

Iran's strategy is to eat away at American power, while legitimising its own role as a regional power with nuclear ambitions. It has been doing so longer than most people remember. As early as 1979, Iran's supreme leader and his acolytes identified Lebanon – a small, diverse country with a sizeable Shia minority – as the most propitious terrain for his grand plans. Lebanon, never a player, always an arena, provided Iran with the perfect foothold on the Mediterranean, and became the place where the greater United Sates–Iran showdown began.

Shifting sands and killing fields

In 1982, Lebanon was five years into a civil war. The summer of 1982 had seen a paroxysm of violence with the Israeli invasion of Lebanon and siege of Beirut; the assassination of Lebanon's president-elect and friend of Israel, Christian Phalangist Bashir Gemayel; and the retaliatory massacres in the Palestinian refugee camps Sabra and Shatila by Gemayel's militia. The US Marines had deployed to Lebanon to oversee the evacuation of the Palestinian Liberation Organization and Palestinian guerrillas from Beirut, and left when their mission was complete – only to redeploy within days, following the assassination and massacre in the Palestinian camp.

There had been a lull in the ferocity of the fighting in the fall with the return of the US Marines, who, along with the French and the Italians, were keeping the peace as part of the Multinational Force (MNF). By early 1983, the MNF had settled into its peace-keeping mission. The marines were on the receiving end of the occasional mortar shell or stray bullet but the fighting across Lebanon had abated to its lowest level since 1975. On 18 April, however, a large car bomb exploded at the US embassy in Beirut, killing sixty-three people, including seventeen Americans. Seven of those killed had been CIA employees, including the head of the Middle East region, Robert Ames, who happened to be at the embassy. A group calling itself the Islamic Jihad (IJ) claimed responsibility. US intelligence had picked up chatter between the Iranian foreign ministry and its embassies in Beirut and Damascus, talking about striking US targets in Beirut. Although circumstantial, the evidence seemed to point to Iran, with the IJ as a proxy or ally. Washington saw this as an isolated incident.

Until then, the Lebanese civil war, in its most stripped-down version, had been an ideological fight between the radical left, supporting the Palestinian cause, and the radical right, dreaming of a Christian nation in Lebanon. Piling on top of the country's own domestic problems from corruption to sectarian divisions, the war had been triggered by the presence of Palestinian guerillas, who launched strikes against Israel, in turn bringing Israeli retaliation against Lebanon. The Palestinians laid down the law with their guns within Lebanon, undermining the already shaky central state authority and bumping against right-wing Christian Phalangists who were also taking up arms.

After the evacuation of the PLO in 1982, the nature and scope of the conflict in Lebanon changed; the ideological sands had shifted. Khomeini had made clear he wanted to export the revolution. Since 1982, there was a growing Iranian presence in Lebanon, mostly in the eastern Beqaa Valley, which had attracted the attention of officials in Washington. Yet its significance was still unclear. The Cold War was in full swing, Eastern Europe was behind the Iron Curtain and Ronald Reagan was singularly focused on confronting Communism by helping the mujahedin in Afghanistan fight against the Soviets. The world was divided into good and evil; whatever Iran was up to felt like a sideshow. But the warning signs were everywhere.

The twenty-third of October, 1983, began as a quiet Sunday morning in Beirut – typical in a war-torn country, where a civil war had been raging since 1975. Sundays were often quiet. Beirutis would go for lunch to their favourite restaurant, stroll on the seaside promenade or drive to their home town for lunch with the extended family. Fresh-faced marines were getting an extra half-hour of sleep in their barracks near the airport – the 6 a.m. staff meeting had been cancelled. The night before, they'd eaten pizza, entertained by a country and western band. A couple of marines were standing guard in front of the barracks, within walking distance of the Mediterranean. Another had sneaked out early for a jog and was on his way back. At 6.22, a speeding yellow Mercedes truck laden with explosives rammed through the fence of the compound and crashed into the atrium of the building. The resulting blast turned the building into a heap of concrete, with charred, dismembered bodies and body parts strewn within the wreckage. Two hundred and forty-one American servicemen were killed – the worst loss of life for the US Marine Corps since Iwo Jima in 1945.

The Reagan administration had been worried that by trying to shore up the Lebanese central government and its Christian president, Amine Gemayel, brother of the assassinated president-elect and Phalangist leader, America was becoming a party in a local feud between Muslims and Christians. The attack against the Marines barracks has always been seen in that light. That perspective is not wrong, but it is not the full story either. Iran was using a much wider lens, looking at the whole regional chessboard.

In 1983, the Iran–Iraq War was in its third year. America's allies in the Gulf, Kuwait and Saudi Arabia, had just poured more than US$20 billion into Iraq's war coffers to help Saddam Hussein fight Khomeini's Iran. America was also aiding Saddam, directly and indirectly. For Khomeini, this meant that America was a target, everywhere. The rivalry between Iran and Saudi Arabia and the wider confrontation between Iran and America was now playing out in Lebanon.

The Iran–Iraq War was a defining decade for the Islamic Republic of Iran. Saddam's invasion of Iran was a gift for the still tenuous hold that Khomeini had on the country. Rallying Iranians around the flag and forcefully closing the ranks helped him solidify his gains and entrench his rule. But the isolation Iran faced during these years as the West and a majority of Arab countries sided with Iraq, arming and funding Saddam, while over a million Iranian soldiers and civilians died, was a painful experience, seared in the psyche of the Iranian population and the leadership. This helps explain the lengths to which Iran goes to build up its defences, including with a nuclear programme and influence in the neighbouring countries it uses as forward bases – more on that later.

And so, far away from Iran's borders, in a Machiavellian asymmetrical move, Tehran dealt a blow against America in Beirut and awaited the response. For days, the Reagan administration debated how and how forcefully to retaliate. Military plans were drawn up for air strikes against Iranian assets in Lebanon's eastern Bekaa Valley. There was talk of a joint military strike with the French, who had also been targeted in Beirut on that fateful October Sunday and lost fifty-eight paratroopers. In the end, they did nothing. In his book *The Twilight War: The Secret History of America's Thirty-Year War with Iran*, David Crist delivers a scathing verdict on Reagan's handling of the aftermath. "Despite his repeated public statements promising to punish those who had perpetrated the attack, Reagan had quietly decided to do nothing in response to an attack that killed more servicemen in a single day than any other since the Second World War."

The lesson was not lost on Khomeini, his entourage and his allies in Lebanon. They had stared down America and won, proving they were a worthy adversary. How much farther could the bayonet go?

Kidnappings and amnesties

In this duel, Iran sees America's allies in the region as rivals for influence, such as Saudi Arabia, or outright enemies, such as Israel. One of the Islamic Republic of Iran's professed ambitions is to help Palestinians liberate land from the "Zionist usurpers" and it pours money into groups such as Hezbollah and Hamas to help advance that goal. Supporting an Arab cause is a convenient ploy to shore up Iran's popularity in the mostly Sunni Arab world. Although there have been periods of secret cooperation and trade between Iran and Israel since 1979, particularly during the Iran–Iraq War, inflammatory anti-Israeli rhetoric reached fever pitch during the presidency of Mahmoud Ahmadinejad, and chants of "Death to Israel" were heard again at the funeral of the Islamic Revolutionary Guard colonel assassinated in Tehran, allegedly by the Mossad, in May of this year.

Iran views Saudi Arabia more as a rival, an extension of America's reach into the Arab world. In the aftermath of the Iranian revolution, Iran and Saudi Arabia – which had been allies and twin pillars in the US policy to contain the Soviet Union – turned into mortal enemies, deploying religion and sectarian identities, Sunni and Shia, to fight each other by proxy from Pakistan to Egypt. The shift was provoked by the rise of Khomeini, who saw himself as a leader not only of Iran, not simply of the Shia community, but of the Muslim nation as a whole, one who could replace the House of Saud – even literally, as Custodians of the Two Holy Mosques, in Mecca and Medina. Historically insecure in its role as leader of the Muslim world, the House of Saud decided to use all means necessary to push back against Khomeini and contain his efforts to export the Iranian revolution. The result has been devastating – not only physically, with violence from the

Iran–Iraq War in the 1980s and the war in Yemen that continues today, but also culturally.

The radical version of state-led Shiism that Khomeini exported into Shia communities transformed them beyond recognition. Meanwhile, as Saudi Arabia tried to outdo Iran in a holier-than-thou competition, the kingdom began feeding a trend of Sunni intolerance and extremism that gave birth to a generation of radical Sunni militants who wreaked havoc – not only in the region, but all the way to the United States, with the attacks of 9/11. The difference between the two camps is that Sunni militants are not state-led entities and see the House of Saud as a target to be deposed, whereas Shia radical militants are vanguards of the Islamic Republic of Iran and answer directly to the Iranian supreme leader.

There would be further tests of American mettle by these Iranian vanguards. On 18 January 1984, Malcolm Kerr, president of the American University of Beirut, had just stepped out of an elevator on campus when two assassins, one holding a gun with a silencer, shot him in the back and ran away before anyone could react. Kerr died almost instantly. Soon after, the local office of the French news agency, Agence France Press, received a telephone call from a man claiming to speak for the Islamic Jihad. "We are responsible for the assassination of the president of the American University of Beirut, who was a victim of the American military presence in Lebanon," said the man. "We also vow that not a single American or Frenchman will remain on this soil." This was the same group that had blown up the US embassy and the Marine barracks – a precursor to Hezbollah. They were now coming after soft targets and cultural symbols of America. President Reagan was still vowing not to be cowed in the wake of this latest anti-American attack – but one month later, every single marine was pulled out of Beirut.

What ensued was a kidnapping spree of Westerners throughout the 1980s – ninety-nine in total, including seventeen Americans. Some were held for eight years; many were tortured or held in horrific conditions, chained to radiators. Their names were in and out of the headlines, from American journalist Terry Anderson to the Anglican church envoy Terry Waite. Some died in captivity, such as William Buckley, CIA station chief in Beirut. The trail always led back to Damascus and Tehran. Some of it was connected more directly to the Saudi–Iran rivalry, like the kidnapping of the Saudi consul in Beirut. In exchange for his release, the Iranians demanded the release of four of their diplomats who had gone missing in Beirut.

A first, seemingly isolated kidnapping had taken place in July 1982, a month into the Israeli siege of Beirut, when the acting president of the American University of Beirut, David Dodge, was snatched off campus in broad daylight. He was released a year later. It's not clear what Iran or Damascus got in exchange, but Tehran had tested the tactic and clearly established that the taking of hostages was a useful pressure tool – if only to dominate the airwaves and American collective consciousness, as they had done for 444 days during the embassy hostage crisis in 1979. Even as the Marines came under attack and then withdrew from Lebanon, the Reagan administration thought it was still dealing with one-off incidents and disparate groups. In fact, there was method behind the apparent madness: a pattern was being established.

In December 1983, Hezbollah and the Iranian-backed Iraqi Shia Da'wa group had carried out a coordinated series of bombings in Kuwait against a variety of targets, including the American and French embassies. The goal was in part to dissuade Kuwait from supporting Iraq in the war against Iran. Seventeen men were put on trial in Kuwait and charged in connection with the bombings;

some were sentenced to death. In Lebanon, Hezbollah threatened to kill the Western hostages they were holding if Kuwait carried out the death sentences. Hezbollah abducted more Westerners in Beirut and carried out repeated hijackings during the 1980s, demanding the release of the "Kuwait 17". Kuwait would not relent. The men unexpectedly regained freedom when Iraq invaded Kuwait and emptied the prisons in 1990.

That year also brought the end of Lebanon's civil war. Washington had quietly acquiesced to a full Syrian takeover of Lebanon in exchange for token Syrian participation in Operation Desert Storm to liberate Kuwait. There were now 35,000 Syrian troops in Lebanon. The price of this *Pax Syriana* in Lebanon seemed worth paying for Washington: the civil war had been going on for too long and its violence and chaos did not fit into the new post–Cold War era and the "new world order" that George H.W. Bush had declared with the liberation of Kuwait. Syria also agreed to participate in the 1991 Madrid peace conference – the first time Syrians had ever sat down for direct talks with Israelis. President Hafez al-Assad posed as the generous facilitator in the release of the remaining Western hostages held in Lebanon by Hezbollah, a group operating in a territory he controlled, answering to Iran, his closest ally. Syria and Iran had hoarded chits; now was the time to cash them in exchange for Lebanon, a coveted prize, a playground where they could continue to negotiate with the West by proxy.

As the guns fell silent and Syrian troops took up positions across the country, Lebanon's warlords donned suits and got a

blanket amnesty in return for handing in their weapons and send-
ing their militiamen home. The Saudis oversaw the process via the
Taif Agreement. There was an asterisk in the fine print, however,
that would turn out to be a Trojan horse: everyone in Lebanon
had to disarm, except the resistance groups fighting the Israeli
occupation of south Lebanon. In the dissipating fog of war, the
real extent of Hezbollah's hold on the Shia community was still
unclear. Traditional Shia notables believed the group was just an
expression of the chaos of the conflict and would disappear in
peacetime. Leftists and communists were still part of the resistance movement against Israel, and there were protests calling for
the end of Iranian influence and the departure of its Revolutionary
Guards. But dissent was snuffed out: Hezbollah imposed itself as
the only fighting force against Israel, eliminating everyone else. So,
despite all the anti-American attacks and internal violence that
Hezbollah and Iran had carried out during the 1980s, the Shia
militia kept its weapons.

The group grew as a military and political power over the
decades, with its members elected to parliament and serving in
the government. Hezbollah provided services from healthcare to
education to its members and the wider Shia community, keeping them beholden to it. Meanwhile, throughout the 1990s, every
round of Israeli–Syrian peace talks was accompanied by a few
Hezbollah rockets lobbed at Israel, a convenient way for Syria
and Iran to raise their price at the negotiating table. Until Israeli
troops withdrew in May 2000, Hezbollah enjoyed wide support
from other Lebanese communities, including Christians, for its
tenacity in fighting Israel's occupation of south Lebanon.

But the group did not lay down its weapons after Israel withdrew. Hezbollah had grown into a state within a state, armed to

the teeth outside the purview of the central authority, which it was slowly undermining. Crucially, Hezbollah answered to the leader of another country – the supreme leader of Iran, now Ali Khamenei. Meanwhile, Iran's ambition went beyond a few square kilometres of land in southern Lebanon.

In 2003, the United States invaded Iraq, and Saddam Hussein's regime collapsed, providing Tehran with the opportunity to aim higher and further, using the playbook it had perfected in Lebanon – hostages and militias.

Axis of misery

Until the 2003 invasion, the 1990s and early 2000s had been the era of engagement and a unipolar world led by the United States, where the values of a liberal global order seemed universal and the progress towards democracy around the globe inevitable. From engaging Russia and paving the way for China to join the World Trade Organization to secret American overtures to Iran's reformist president Mohammad Khatami, diplomacy was everywhere. Even Saudi Arabia and Iran had made up, suddenly united in their fear of Saddam Hussein's follies. Diplomatic relations between the two countries had resumed, the détente ushering in an era of relative quiet and prosperity to the region. Khatami introduced the concept of a Dialogue Among Civilizations, to contrast Samuel Huntington's Clash of Civilizations.

But on June 1996, a powerful blast ripped through the Khobar Towers in Dhahran in Saudi Arabia, killing nineteen American Air Force personnel being housed there and wounding more than 400 people. The fingers pointed first at al-Qaeda but suspicion quickly turned to a pro-Iran Shia group, Hezbollah al Hejaz, affiliated with Lebanon's Hezbollah and several Shia operatives from Saudi Arabia and Lebanon. Iran had struck two goals in one: the near enemy, Saudi Arabia, and the far enemy, America, conveniently available as a target on Saudi soil. Despite this, the Saudis were reluctant to condemn Iran, and engagement continued. US president Bill Clinton made a secret overture to President Khatami in 1999 but was rebuffed.

Mohammed al Sulami, a Saudi expert on Iran, told me that, in hindsight, it was clear that the Islamic Revolutionary Guard Corps (IRGC) was biding its time. The paramilitary group was using this period of détente to continue entrenching its networks across the region, including in Lebanon, but also as far away as Africa, often in the guise of cultural and religious activities, hiding behind the moderate face of Khatami. It was also during this period that Iran began to build its secret nuclear programme.

When the United States invaded Iraq in 2003, Iran was unleashed – its western border nemesis, Saddam Hussein, was gone. Barely two years earlier, its enemy to the east, the Taliban, had also been removed. America had unwittingly provided Iran with the space and opportunity to spread its wings across the region. Iran set out to change the score of the Iran–Iraq War, which had essentially ended in stalemate in 1988, with an unsatisfactory ceasefire that Khomeini had described as a poisoned chalice. Iran could now work to take over Iraq's politics, economy and society in an effort to turn Iraq into a vassal state. In doing so, it would achieve another goal: thwarting American power.

In the immediate aftermath of the invasion, America and the West's focus was on the Sunni insurgency. The Iraqi franchise of al-Qaeda, run by Abu Musab al-Zarqawi, was carrying out spectacular attacks, starting with the October 2003 bombing of the

UN headquarters in Baghdad that killed the UN special representative Sérgio Vieira de Mello and twenty-one others. Although Iran and al-Qaeda are ostensibly enemies, Iran saw an advantage in facilitating al-Qaeda violence in Iraq, including by giving refuge to some of Osama bin Laden's relatives and providing the group with technical expertise. Meanwhile, Syria allowed jihadis from around the world to cross through its territory into Iraq, feeding the fire of the insurgency. More than 4000 US troops have been killed in Iraq since 2003, and over 30,000 wounded. "Given Iran's fear that the US planned to use a successful, democratic Iraq as a platform to subvert or threaten Iran, the Islamic Republic sought to turn Iraq into an inferno," said Karim Sadjadpour from the Carnegie Endowment for International Peace.

The IRGC was also busy training and arming Shia militias in Iraq, leveraging the networks within the Iraqi Shia opposition that had been in exile in Iran during the Saddam years and had returned home after the fall of the dictator. An estimated 500 of the American soldiers killed in Iraq died in attacks carried out using Iranian weapons or improvised explosive devices made by Iran or Iranian-backed Shia militias in Iraq. "For years, the US saw Iran as a straightforward terrorist threat, not as a regional threat. The aftermath of the Iraq War in 2003 changed that," said Michael Singh.

Tehran's first lesson from its Lebanon playbook was that it could push American troops out of a territory if it used enough violence to make the deployment costly, and difficult for Americans to stomach. The pressure on America to withdraw from Iraq grew as the casualty toll rose and in 2008, President Obama campaigned on a promise to end the war in Iraq.

"What Iran's leaders learned in Lebanon in the 1980s," said Sadjadpour,

> was that killing American soldiers in the Middle East has a profound impact on American public opinion, which then diminishes American resolve to maintain its presence in conflict zones. If you attack Americans in New York City, the American public will support a retaliation; if you kill American soldiers in the Middle East the more common popular reaction is "why are our boys dying in these dangerous faraway places?"

Obama withdrew all combat forces in 2011. Meanwhile, Iran was overpowering Iraq, funding and arming Shia militias, evading US sanctions by siphoning off Iraqi oil, and pushing its friends into key positions across all sectors of Iraq's politics and economy as well as into the religious seminaries.

In 2014, Obama was forced to send American troops back to Iraq to lead the coalition against the Islamic State, which had taken over large swathes of western Iraq and north-western Syria. Iran perceived the instability ISIS created in Iraq as a direct threat, in part because of ISIS's avowed anti-Shia and anti-Iran positions and the associated danger for the Shia holy sites of Najaf and Kerbala in Iraq. Iran reacted by positioning itself as part of the wide effort against ISIS and was briefly seen as unofficial partner in the coalition – US planes fought ISIS in the air and Iranian-backed Shia militias fought on the ground, under the leadership of Quds Force commander Qassem Soleimani.

Najaf's leading clerical authority, Ayatollah Ali al-Sistani, had called on Iraqis of all faiths to take up arms against ISIS, under the umbrella of the national army. Iran seized on the movement and took over, resulting in a parallel Shia army, known as the Popular Mobilization Forces, grouping several dozen militant groups, with anywhere between 60,000 and 140,000 fighters. ISIS is (mostly) gone but the PMF remains, answering for the most part directly to Tehran and the supreme leader. Across the border in Syria, the IRGC and Hezbollah control territory in support of President Assad. Hezbollah also controls many of the levers of political and economic life in the diverse, multi-sectarian Lebanon, which has been slowly strangled by the group's power and its alliance with a corrupt ruling establishment.

As American administrations come and go, and policies towards Iran change, from calling for engagement and understanding Iran's grievances to exerting maximum pressure, Iran stays the course, working diligently to gain ground and expand its reach. Today, Khamenei presides over what Sadjadpour describes as an axis of misery, from Yemen to Iraq, Syria to Lebanon – countries which, as Iran's control over them grows, have become mired in violence and unrest, with militias running amok, power cuts and bread lines, and a massive brain drain.

In November 2021, I spoke to an Iranian professor who lives in Tehran and is close to the regime's thinking. He shared his thoughts candidly, preferring to remain anonymous. I asked him: what was Iran's vision for these countries, what was Tehran offering? I expected the usual rhetoric about Iranian support for the oppressed with funding for schools and healthcare, or the defence of Shia shrines in Iraq and Syria, or even the usual propaganda about the valiant militias defending Muslim rights against attacks from the Zionist enemy. Instead, I got the most honest, straight-forward answer I had ever heard from an Iranian: Iraq, Lebanon, Syria and Yemen, he said, "serve as forward defence bases for Iran", a way to ensure the survival of the Iranian regime by providing a protective ring around its territory, with weapons and loyal foot soldiers that keep Iran's enemies busy far from its own borders.

The second part of Iran's Lebanon playbook was that taking hostages allows it to hoard chits in advance of any negotiations. No matter how Iran characterises the imprisonment of Iranian dual citizens in its jails – charging them with espionage or other trumped-up accusations, for example – the only word to describe these prisoners is "hostages". From *Washington Post* correspondent Jason Rezaian to British-Iranian Nazanin Zaghari-Ratcliffe, who was released as part of a larger deal that included the release of Iranian funds, to Iranian-American businessman Siamak Namazi, who continues to languish in jail along with many others, the tactic of holding prisoners/hostages has become state policy, part of the toolbox Iran uses to negotiate with the West.

One further lesson Iran has learnt to ensure regime survival came from watching the downfall of Libya's Muammar al-Gaddafi: give up your weapons of mass destruction and you lose leverage, protection and deterrence. The isolation and destruction wrought on Iran in the 1980s during the war with Iraq has not been for-gotten, and the fear of Western designs for regime change in Iran explains Tehran's pursuit of a nuclear programme. One could also look at Ukraine today – if it hadn't transferred Soviet nuclear weap-ons and stations on its territory to Russia after the fall of the Soviet Union, Putin might have thought twice about invading. There is a counter-argument, of course: that the mere suspicion of the pres-ence of weapons of mass destruction or a nuclear programme can provide a casus belli, as in the case of Iraq in 2003. Iran is likely betting that neither the United States nor Israel will do more than sabotage operations, including the assassination of scientists.

Iran's forward bases also provide necessary resources and territory to feed its coffers, whether from Iraqi oil or illicit trade across Lebanon and Syria, including drugs. Tehran has an almost uninterrupted territorial corridor, through Iraq and Syria all the way to Lebanon, to facilitate the flow of arms to Shia militias. It's in these forward bases that those who do not subscribe to the Islamic Republic of Iran's worldview attempt to forge a different path – often at great risk to themselves.

Killing the alternative

The list of assassinations that have been blamed on Iran and its proxies is long – from Lebanon's former prime minister Rafic al-Hariri, killed in 2005 in a massive blast, to Hisham al-Hashimi, Iraqi historian, security researcher and adviser to Iraqi prime minister Mustafa al-Kadhimi, shot dead in 2020 in Baghdad. A string of assassinations in Lebanon from 2005 to 2006 seemed designed to pick off enough anti-Hezbollah MPs to change the majority in favour of the Shia group.

In late 2013, Mohammad Chatah, former ambassador of Lebanon to the United States, former finance minister and an adviser to the prime minister, Saad al-Hariri, son of the murdered Hariri, was pinning his hopes on diplomacy and engagement. Hassan Rouhani had just been elected president in Iran, secret talks between Tehran and the Obama administration had been revealed and the interim nuclear accord had just been reached in Geneva. There seemed to be an opportunity for a new, more

positive relationship between Iran and the West, and a softer
Iranian approach to the region. Chatah penned an open letter to
Rouhani, appealing to him to chart a new course for Iran in its
relationship with his country, Lebanon – one that allowed state
institutions and national unity to thrive. "Hezbollah continues to
maintain an independent and heavily armed military force outside
the authority of the state. This is happening with the direct support
and sponsorship of your country," wrote the veteran politician. "As
we are sure you would agree, [this] is not only in conflict with the
Lebanese constitution, but also with the very definition of a sovereign state – any state."

At the beginning of 2013, Hezbollah had begun to send fighters across the border to Syria to assist President Bashar al-Assad
in his efforts to crush the rebellion against him. The uprising had
started in 2011 as a peaceful movement against an oppressive dictator but it was descending into a chaotic civil war. Chatah called
into question Hezbollah's unilateral decision-making on matters
of war and peace, saying it endangered Lebanon's stability and
risked dragging the country into the war. In addressing Hezbollah's
sponsor in Tehran, Chatah laid out four steps to help shore up
Lebanon's stability and sovereignty, starting with a declaration
of Lebanese neutrality and the end of all armed participation by
Lebanese groups, including Hezbollah, in the Syrian conflict. Even
more daringly, he called for full control of the Lebanese army over
the border with Syria, across which Hezbollah fighters flow into
Syria and weapons from Iran flow into Lebanon – all through
illegal crossings. Finally, he called on the UN Security Council
to declare the interim cessation of hostilities with Israel a permanent ceasefire, effectively eliminating the reason for Hezbollah to
remain armed under the guise of resistance against Israel.

Chatah was looking to gather signatures from members of Lebanon's parliament for his letter to present it to Rouhani. On 27 November 2013, he tweeted: "As Iran ends its nuclear winter & promises an economic spring should Lebanon languish as host to the Levant Subsidiary of Iran's Resistance?" On 27 December, at 9.40 a.m., Chatah was killed when a bomb exploded in a parked car in downtown Beirut. The site of the attack was barely a five-minute walk from where Chatah's previous boss, Rafic the father, had been assassinated on Valentine's Day 2005 in a massive, sophisticated car bomb. Chatah had been prescient: after 2013, Hezbollah's role expanded further into a regional paramilitary force with foot soldiers deployed as far away as Yemen.

Four decades into exporting Iran's revolution, the project requires constant force to be maintained

By 2019, Iran's power had expanded considerably when a wave of protests erupted in Iraq and Lebanon. The target was the corrupt sectarian establishment in each country, which was driving up unemployment, draining resources, leaving citizens in the dark – literally – allowing militias to thrive, filling their pockets and giving jobs to their friends while generally failing to deliver for their citizens. In Lebanon, it was the start of one of the worst financial and economic crises in the world in the last 150 years, according to the World Bank. In both countries, the target of the anger was also Iran's hold on their politics and economy and Iran's support for armed groups that undermine and hollow out the state. The anti-Iran anger was most vocal in Iraq and included Shia clerics taking to the streets with banners demanding an end to Iranian interference. In Lebanon, where Hezbollah had long posed as a rightful resistance movement – an opposition party fighting corruption and upholding the rights of the poor and the Shia community – the facade no longer held. The party benefited from the corrupt system and protected it. This eruption of popular anger, in parallel with protests in Iran itself, was likely one of the most complex challenges that the Islamic Republic of Iran had faced in years, the clearest sign that, four decades into exporting Iran's revolution, the project requires constant force to be maintained.

Lebanese and Iraqi protestors were met with violence from the local Iran-backed Shia militias or, in Lebanon's case, their front men and local thugs. "We in Iran know how to deal with protestors," Quds Force commander Soleimani reportedly told Iraqi officials when the protests started. "This happened in Iran and we got it under control." More than 500 Iraqis were killed, many shot dead by snipers, men in black operating outside the purview of state authority and most likely answering to the IRGC. In Lebanon, the violence was more measured but just as effective. Hezbollah stayed in the background but relied on an entourage of loyal thugs to go out with clubs, shoving and beating protestors and burning down the tents they had erected in downtown Beirut. The start of the pandemic in March 2020 was a convenient excuse to send the protesters home. As Iraq and Lebanon geared up for parliamentary elections – October 2021 for Iraq and May 2022 for Lebanon – a string of assassinations targeted promising candidates, journalists and activists who were putting forward an alternative vision for their country. In Lebanon, the prominent Shia intellectual and writer Lokman Slim was shot dead in February 2021.

Although Iran's allies in both Iraq and Lebanon ended up losing their parliamentary majorities in the elections, Mahmoud

Sariolghalam, an Iranian political scientist and adviser to Iranian officials such as Rouhani, believes there is very little in the domestic political mechanisms of countries like Iraq and Lebanon that allows people to outmanoeuvre Tehran. Even as a minority group in parliament, Hezbollah has enough power that it can be a spoiler, blocking the formation of a cabinet or the election of a new president, and stalling any reforms that don't suit its agenda. Challenging Iran's grip will have to be part of a regional and international approach, through a concerted pressure campaign on Iran combined with assertive diplomacy, which would require close cooperation between Saudi Arabia and the United States. Ronnie Chatah, son of the assassinated Chatah and a friend of Slim, once told me that there had to be a way, through diplomacy, to convince Iran that Hezbollah was not essential to the survival of the regime in Tehran. No one has cracked that code yet.

When Iranian officials boast that Iran controls four capitals – Beirut, Baghdad, Damascus and Sana'a – it is a statement not only

Iran continues to insist that its nuclear programme is civilian and peaceful

about the failure of Arab leadership but also about the failure of America to support its allies and shape the course of political events. Prodding with a bayonet around the region, Iran encounters a combination of disorganised, disunited Arab regional polity, Israeli military and covert actions, and American policymakers who often see Iran purely as a terrorist threat, rather than a regional player, and are focused on the danger of its nuclear ambitions. In between these three poles lies wide spaces for Iran to chip away at American power in the region, including through nuclear talks.

Nukes and uprisings

Iran's civilian nuclear programme dates back to the 1950s, when the Shah and the United States were friends. Iran signed the Non-Proliferation Treaty in 1968 and the United States supplied Iran with enriched uranium for its nuclear power plants – until 1979. Post-Shah, as an Islamic Republic, Iran received assistance from Russia and China for its civilian nuclear programme. In 2002, an Iranian opposition group revealed secret nuclear facilities inside Iran, raising suspicion about a possible nuclear weapons programme supported by Pakistan and North Korea. Over the next decade, efforts to engage Iran in negotiations and bring it into compliance with international protocols mostly ended in failure. Iran's nuclear programme grew extensively: from trying to assemble 164 uranium-enrichment centrifuges to having 18,000 centrifuges spinning across the country; from a nascent programme to seventeen declared nuclear sites, including a heavy water reactor. Iran continues to insist that its nuclear programme is civilian and peaceful.

Finally, in November 2013, a breakthrough initial nuclear agreement was clinched in Geneva between Iran and the P5+1 (the UN's Security Council's five permanent members plus Germany) after several rounds of negotiations. It was quickly revealed that months of secret negotiations between Obama administration officials and Iranian officials since summer 2012, mostly held in Oman, had been crucial in laying the groundwork for the accord. Saudi Arabia was stunned into silence by the revelation, while Israel's prime minister, Benjamin Netanyahu, criticised the deal with his customary hyperbole. "Today," he warned, "the world has become a much more dangerous place because the most dangerous regime in the world has taken a significant step toward attaining the most dangerous weapon in the world." The combination of Iran's anti-Israel rhetoric and a rapidly advancing nuclear programme is seen as an existential threat by many Israelis, but Netanyahu's criticism of the nuclear deal is not shared by everyone – many Israeli defence and intelligence officials maintain that any deal is better than no deal.

The benefits of the negotiations and the final nuclear deal – known as the Joint Comprehensive Plan of Action (JCPOA), signed in Vienna in July 2015 – were undeniable from a proliferation perspective. Iran agreed, among other things, to serious constraints on its nuclear programme by reducing or eliminating stockpiles of medium- and low-enriched uranium, limiting the enrichment of further uranium to a percentage sufficient only for civilian nuclear power, and placing two-thirds of its centrifuges in storage. Nuclear experts critiquing the deal focused on the sunset clauses, which meant that the restrictions would expire after eight, ten or fifteen years, leaving Iran free to resume its nuclear programme.

Middle East experts also warned that nuclear negotiators were too narrowly focused on the nuclear program and disregarded the extent to which the region had changed between the first secret meeting in Oman – in the summer of 2012 – and the moment the JCPOA was signed in 2015, a period during which Iran had extensively expanded its reach and power across the region.

In 2012, the peaceful uprising in Syria against Assad was just a year old but starting to turn bloody, and unrest in Yemen was still focused on efforts to get rid of the regime of Ali Abdullah Saleh. Although Iran's supreme leader, Ali Khamenei, had declared the Arab uprisings to be Islamic awakenings that followed in the footsteps of Iran's own Islamic revolution, the spontaneous outpouring of protestors onto the streets of Tunis, Cairo, Benghazi and Damascus was an expression of decades of frustrations against oppression and dictatorship, not of a desire to follow Iran's example.

But Tehran sensed an opportunity amid the upheaval, inserting itself where it could. By 2015, it was firmly entrenched on the ground in Syria, deploying the IRGC's Quds Force as well as Hezbollah militants to help prop up Assad. In Yemen, the Houthis, an Islamist radical militant movement from the Zaydi branch of Shiism, had taken over the capital. Though Houthi links to Iran were initially limited, the group was emulating Lebanon's Hezbollah. Saudi Arabia saw an immediate Iranian threat on its border and launched a war to quash the movement and reclaim Sana'a. And yet, throughout the nuclear negotiations, American officials stayed focused solely on the details of proliferation. When faced with the angst of the Gulf monarchies and particularly Saudi Arabia, which was starting to feel encircled by Iran, President Barack Obama had nothing to offer.

In his view, "most of the destabilising activity that Iran engages in is low-tech, low-cost activity" – in other words, it didn't seem much to worry about. He advised Gulf countries to ramp up their own asymmetric warfare to challenge Iran. What happened instead was the world's worst humanitarian crisis, in Yemen. Seven years since the start of the Saudi-led war against the Houthis, Iranian and Hezbollah influence in Yemen and support for the Houthis has deepened, while the fighting is mostly at a stalemate – despite US support for the Saudi war efforts, especially early on in the war. The nuclear deal was therefore sealed just as Iran felt emboldened regionally and was suddenly also flush with cash from the lifting of sanctions.

Ballast

Whenever countries like Iran give up something, it's always worth pausing to ask why. Are they just throwing ballast overboard to stay afloat? Giving up a chit that matters tremendously to their opponent but not much to them? Did Iran actually want a nuclear programme that could eventually be weaponised and, if so, why did it agree to the limitations imposed by the nuclear deal?

The aftermath of the Hariri assassination in 2005 illustrates this well. Hariri had clashed with his overlords in Damascus and was trying to wriggle out from under the *Pax Syriana* that had brought an end to the civil war in 1990. He was killed for it, but his death brought massive protests that led to huge popular and international pressure on Syria to withdraw its 35,000 troops from Lebanon. A UN tribunal would later charge at least one Hezbollah operative with planning and carrying out the assassination. Syria appeared to have blinked and its withdrawal seemed to usher in a new dawn for Lebanon, one in which Syrian and Iranian influence would wane and progressive, democratic forces would take the country forward. But the hope was short-lived. Syrian soldiers went home but left behind a well-oiled, decades-old machine of intelligence operatives and allies that still served Damascus. Crucially, Hezbollah's power, backed by its arsenal of weapons, was intact. Damascus and Iran had given up something they no longer needed – a physical Syrian armed presence in Lebanon. In doing so, they had defused international pressure and ensured the survival of the Syrian regime itself.

> *Ever since the revolution, this Iranian regime has been consistent and predictable in its anti-American, anti-Western policies*

So, why did Iran agree to the 2015 nuclear deal? In Washington, positive-thinking diplomats were hoping that engagement with Iran would empower its more centrist president, Hassan Rouhani, and his entourage, and help soften its position in the region, bringing it into the Western fold. One senior American official told me that, thanks to its history and culture, Iran had more potential for becoming a democracy in the long term than a country like Saudi Arabia. But they seem to overlook that ever since the revolution, this Iranian regime has been consistent and predictable in its anti-American, anti-Western policies.

For Iran, the 2015 nuclear deal was a necessary release valve at a time when tensions with the United States had been rising, domestic discontent had been bubbling up and the sanctions were taking their toll. Khamenei and his entourage may even have paved the way for the victory of Rouhani as president in 2013, to take over from the bombastic ideologue, Mahmoud Ahmadinejad, specifically to continue the engagement with the United States, which had started in 2012. The charms of Rouhani's smooth-talking foreign minister, Javad Zarif, were the perfect antithesis to Ahmadinejad's anti-American railings and helped feed expectations in Washington of a wider détente. Iran went on a charm offensive, welcoming Western reporters into the country. But one of the American negotiators, a non-proliferation expert focused on the nitty-gritty of the accord, remained clear-eyed. "Whenever I sit with a smiling Javad Zarif, I imagine Qassem Soleimani standing behind him in the corner," he told me in 2015.

After the JCPOA was signed, Iranians celebrated the possibility of rejoining the international community. The euphoria was short-lived – and not only because President Donald Trump withdrew from the agreement. Even before Obama's term ended,

Iran complained that the windfall from the lifting of sanctions was limited because other terrorism-related sanctions remained in place, scaring away banks and international companies. Iran's economy and oil industry lagged, weighed down by years of sanctions, corruption and the IRGC's hold over all sectors, its hands in the piggy bank. On a reporting trip to Tehran in the summer of 2015, just months after the deal was announced in Vienna, I found a mix of hope and despondency, between eagerness to connect with the world and a reflexive defensive crouch. I wrote then about the expected collision between the hopes of a young population eager to seize a once-in-a-generation opportunity and a conservative ideological leadership that had opened the door just enough to let some air in and deflate domestic criticism, but whose survival depended on maintaining its anti-American posture.

In 2018, Sariolghalam, the Iranian political scientist, wrote in an essay: "anti-Americanism continues to serve as the raison d'être of the Islamic Republic of Iran. This has less to do with the nature of the American system and more to do with the fact that Iran has turned anti-Americanism into an identity." In other words, even if the United States had lifted all sanctions, even if Trump had not withdrawn from the nuclear deal, Khamenei would look to provoke new sanctions and continued enmity with the United States.

Legitimacy

And yet, despite Ayatollah Khomeini's pronouncement that Iran "will resist America until our last breath", his regime does seek the legitimacy that dealing with America or besting America can bestow. For Singh, "the original nuclear deal in 2015 wasn't just about sanctions relief (for Iran), it helped to legitimise the Iranian nuclear programme and end Iranian isolation".

This is apparent again in the nuclear talks now taking place in Vienna. Biden administration officials are having to negotiate via their allies in the P5+1 because Iranians will not meet directly with Americans, showing they can dictate the rules of engagement with the world's superpower.

When Joe Biden was elected president, Tehran rejoiced, believing that he would be eager to return to the nuclear deal his former boss had signed, and that he would quickly agree to lift all sanctions in exchange for Iran coming back into compliance with the JCPOA. It was an easy miscalculation: aside from Biden himself, the new administration included many familiar faces from the Obama administration, such as Jake Sullivan, who was one of the secret negotiators in 2012 and is now Biden's national security adviser. Bill Burns, then deputy secretary of state, also travelled to Oman and is now the CIA chief. One of Iran's favourite interlocutors, Robert Malley, was part of Obama's negotiating team and is now leading the talks with Iran. Across the region, Iran's allies and proxies anticipated fresh cash and a free rein, as the Biden administration seemed to signal it was also disengaging from the region. Saudi analysts flippantly disparaged the "Obama bros", whom they accused of readying to hand over the Middle East to Iran.

More than a year into the Biden administration, at the time of writing, there is still no nuclear deal. Meanwhile, according to a March report by the International Atomic Energy Agency, Iran is now enriching uranium to 60 per cent purity and its stock of enriched uranium stands at 3.2 tonnes, meaning the country is getting ever closer to becoming a nuclear threshold state. In June,

Iran upped the ante by turning off twenty-seven surveillance cameras placed by the IAEA in nuclear sites.

Reading the tea leaves of American foreign policy requires an understanding of the people at its heart who might operate differently depending on which president they are serving and where they feature in the hierarchy. Obama's aides included people such as deputy national security adviser Benjamin Rhodes and White House chief of staff Denis McDonough, who shared his worldview. But Sullivan and Burns were in a different orbit. Sullivan had risen through the ranks of the foreign policy machine as Hillary Clinton's adviser, while Burns is a career diplomat with one of the sharpest minds in Washington and no illusions about the ability of the Iranian regime and Vladimir Putin's to cause havoc. From the outset, Biden made clear to his team he was opposed to the blanket lifting of sanctions. In addition, Sullivan had spoken during the election campaign about the need to make the deal longer and stronger, in reference to the sunset clauses approaching expiration as well as addressing Iran's ballistic missile programme and its regional behaviour. The presence of Rob Malley as the key negotiator obscured these more pragmatic views.

Iran kept prodding with a bayonet – thinking it would find mush among the "Obama bros"

After its initial disappointment that Biden did not rush to return to the prior agreement, Iran elected as president Ebrahim Raissi – a hardline cleric, known as the hanging judge for his role as one of the four judges who oversaw the torture and executions of an estimated 5000 people in 1988. The analysis on the left in the United States was that the moderates in Iran had lost, unable to show what was to gain from engaging with America, and that the election result therefore was a reaction to America's intransigence. A more accurate read is that Khamenei no longer had any use for the moderates. "Iran stops pretending", the headline of an *Atlantic* article by Karim Sadjadpour, was the perfect summation.

But Iran kept prodding with a bayonet – thinking it would find mush among the "Obama bros". And while Tehran had always insisted that no regional issues should be put on the table in the nuclear negotiations, it suddenly requested that the Biden administration lift the designation of the IRGC as a foreign terrorist organisation. The Trump administration had formally made the designation in 2019, mostly a symbolic move; the more devastating blow to Iran was the January 2020 American strike that killed Soleimani. But the political fallout of removing the IRGC from the list would be immense, even if the designation made little difference to its ability to operate. America would send a terrible signal to its jittery allies in the region by rewarding Iran without any meaningful improvement in its behaviour. Even worse, it would have come at a time when Iran has been upping the pressure on the negotiators in Vienna via proxy attacks on US troops in Iraq.

Although Iran appeared to make this a condition sine qua non for progressing and concluding the deal, the talks did not collapse when it became clear that President Biden would not budge. In essence, Washington had called Tehran's bluff. But why did Iran even include this item on the agenda? According to Singh, the "Iranians wanted to be able to claim a success beyond the nuclear deal and send out a message that they had prevailed in staring down the US, despite the maximum pressure of sanctions". But Iran had miscalculated. It found a more steadfast and inflexible position than it had been accustomed to in its decades of dealing with America, of negotiating and attacking at the same time.

Order from chaos

Looking back over decades of Iran's machinations around the region in pursuit of its singular goal of pushing America out of the Middle East, the question is: how should the West show steel to Iran's bayonet without feeding endless confrontation or going down the dangerous road of regime change? And how should those who live in Iran's sphere of influence deal with its efforts to subjugate them, short of capitulation?

According to Sadjadpour, "Iran is arguably the most powerful country in the region today, but their power is almost entirely dedicated to destruction rather than construction. Aside from militias, they don't really build anything; they exacerbate chaos and power vacuums and fight American influence."

Tehran is hoping that Russia and China are its allies in the endeavour of pushing out America. Both alliances have limitations. In Syria, Russia's use of military force and air power to help shore up Assad's regime demonstrated that Iran and Hezbollah on their own were not able to truly grant Assad a decisive victory over the civilian revolutionaries and armed rebels that have been fighting his rule since 2011. This means that although Iran is deeply entrenched in Syria, it is the junior partner in a marriage of convenience with Russia. It also has to contend with Russia's unofficial green light to Israeli air strikes that target Iranian assets in Syria. As Russia sinks deeper into the Ukraine war, Iran must be both hoping that Moscow will be less physically present in Syria and worried this might give breathing room to the anti-Assad protests that continue to simmer under the surface.

When it comes to China, Iran misunderstands Beijing's goals and overestimates its desire to stare down America. While China would like to reduce American power around the world, if not replace it, the Middle East is one region where it benefits from American underwriting of the security structure and the stability this brings to oil markets. Tehran may boast about signing a multi-billion-dollar memorandum of understanding with Beijing, but Beijing is much cozier with Saudi Arabia and Iraq, its two top oil suppliers. China has never dipped its toes into Middle East politics and prefers to leave the frustrating exercise of dealmaking and peacemaking in the region to the United States, from Iraqi government formations to the Israeli–Palestinian conflict. Furthermore, Iran's funding of militias in Iraq, its backing of the Houthis, and the drone and missile attacks against oil facilities in Saudi Arabia and against the UAE all add volatility to the oil market, which does not suit China. American and Chinese interest in the Middle East are more aligned than Iran realises.

In January 2020, a senior Saudi official told me that the best way to confront Iran was to offer a positive economic model that would counter Iran's trail of devastation, eating away at its system of patronage. Considering Saudi Arabia's own devastating record in Yemen, its decades of chequebook diplomacy feeding corruption and individual politicians instead of building institutions, and its growing internal repression, the kingdom is not well placed to speak of positive economic models. And although the social and cultural transformation of the kingdom in the last couple of years under Mohammed bin Salman have been tremendous, it does not have the capacity or ability to implement a regional vision – certainly not on its own. But the overall diagnosis is correct: if Iran benefits from disorder, then order makes it more difficult for Tehran to thrive as a regional power. Recent efforts at regional economic cooperation, especially on energy issues, seem designed to deliver on that – from Saudi Arabia investing in Iraq's energy sector, to Jordan, Israel and the UAE signing a renewable energy deal, to Egypt and Jordan providing gas to Lebanon. The Trump administration saw the Abraham Accords as a way to bring Arabs and Israelis together in opposition to Iran. In the absence of a nuclear deal, the Biden administration may try to expand the accords, although Saudi Arabia will not take any significant public steps towards Israel if there is no movement in the Israeli–Palestinian conflict or improvement of Palestinian life under Israeli occupation. The Biden administration is also hampered by its tense relationship with Saudi Arabia. As a presidential candidate, Biden called the kingdom a pariah after the murder of Saudi journalist Jamal Khashoggi in a Saudi consulate in Istanbul in 2018. Finding a way to mend ties while holding Saudi Arabia accountable would fit into a larger effort to put forward a constructive, positive vision for the region's future.

In 2019, Jake Sullivan, now President Biden's national security adviser, wrote in *The Atlantic* that "the U.S. needs to adopt the foreign-policy version of the serenity prayer: Grant us the wisdom to know the difference between those things we can change and those we cannot." The United States cannot and should not change the Iranian regime, but it can work with America's partners to deny Tehran the chaos it seeks – and to provide the people of the Middle East a viable alternative to Iran's axis of misery. ≡

Itamar Ben-Avi's search for autonomy

Arie M. Dubnov

Like most Jewish Israelis of my generation, I was familiar with the name Itamar Ben-Avi first and foremost thanks to his role as the "son of": he was born Itamar Ben-Zion (literally "son of Zion"), the eldest son of Deborah and Eliezer Ben-Yehuda, the famous Zionist lexicographer and journalist who acquired, rightly or wrongly, the status of "reviver" of the Hebrew language as a modern vernacular. It was from his entrepreneurial, restless father, who founded several newspapers and associations to spread his views in favour of national and linguistic renewal, that Itamar Ben-Avi learned the power of the written word and the importance of the free press. Yet Ben-Yehuda senior was also a short-tempered and exceedingly strict parent. He treated his firstborn as part of his cultural nation-building project, homeschooling him and prohibiting contact with other children to make him the first Ashkenazi child to speak uncontaminated modern Hebrew. The experiment yielded the expected results: at the age of three, Itamar uttered his first word, *aba* (father); at eleven years old, he sent Lord Rothschild a letter notifying him about his plans to establish a Hebrew army; and when he was fifteen years old, he launched his own Hebrew-language newspaper, called *Hayeled* ("The Child"), which his parents, unhappy with its contents, closed down after its first issue.

We learned about this youthful melodrama in elementary school, from *Ha-Bechor Le-Beit Avi* (translated as *Rebirth: The Story of Eliezer Ben-Yehudah and the Modern Hebrew Language*), a sanitised version of the story produced by Dvora Omer, a popular children's novelist, which entered school curricula and remains in circulation to this day. Omer's sentimental, though somewhat preachy, account of the child blossoming to maturity meant to inculcate in us, the pupils, the correct ideological messages: continue the courageous struggles for a Hebrew language and culture, away from the customs of the *Galut* and the philanthropy-dependent "old *Yishuv*", and the ongoing effort to forge a new and independent Hebrew subject, bold and proud. Itamar Ben-Avi, in other words, was the epitome of the native-born Palestinian Jew, a Sabra before the term was even thought of, who personified the shift of authority away from the sacred scripture to the spoken Hebrew of the native-born. These were the materials from which the great Zionist family drama was made.

Itamar Ben-Avi would spend much of his adult career as a journalist, and, like his father, he coined numerous words that are still in use in contemporary Hebrew. A partial list includes the Hebrew words for statesman (*medinai*), armoured vehicle (*meshurian*), budget (*takziv*), telegram (*mivrak*), greenhouse (*hamama*), defeatism (*tvustanut*) and even contemporary (*akhshavi*). He also coined the Hebrew term *atzmaut* (עצמאות). But what was *atzmaut*? Most dictionaries would translate the word as independence: the state of being not dependent, a condition of being free from external control. But was this really what Ben-Avi meant?

Many years after elementary school, already a parent myself, I picked up Ben-Avi's posthumously published memoir. Cryptically titled *Im Shachar Atzma'utenu* (*With the Dawn of Our Atzmaut*), it described the pressures placed on him by his demanding father with his strict didacticism and constant attempts to evade societal pressures, and his struggle to forge his own individuality, independent style and desires. The memoir was the Hebrew equivalent of John Stuart Mill's famous autobiography, and I realised that beneath the filial admiration, it highlighted Ben-Avi's struggle for autonomy, free from the yoke of the much-revered authority figure, and weaved his own story with that of the Jewish national movement, just as Mill made his personal emancipation story a platform on which he later placed his liberal philosophy. And yet even the pen name he adopted – Ben-Avi, constructed from an acronym of his father's name – expressed a filial devotion. The word *atzmaut* – derived from the Hebrew word for self (*atzmi*, עצמי) – featured in the title of his autobiographical Zionist *bildungsroman*, a narration of Ben-Avi's journey to find his "self".

After a short stint as a teacher in Jaffa, Ben-Avi started his journalistic career early, as an editor at his father's newspapers. He witnessed, with much enthusiasm, albeit from a provincial distance, the late-Ottoman *Tanzimat* reforms and the emergence of the Arab *Nahda* ("awakening"), which led to mass readership and the creation of distribution channels for printed texts. He made his first professional steps as a participant in this vibrant intellectual scene and, like his father, embraced the 1908 Young Turk Revolution. "Never was the Messiah so close, so dependent on our deeds, as he is today," Eliezer Ben-Yehuda wrote in his newspaper *Ha-Tsvi*, calling upon his fellow Jews, the majority of whom were foreign nationals, to acquire Ottoman citizenship and enfranchisement. (The Zionist Palestine Office estimated there were between 45,000 to 50,000 Jews living in Jerusalem in the early twentieth century, whereas the US Consulate in Jerusalem estimated their number reached 60,000. However, the 1905 Ottoman census counted only 13,441 Jews with Ottoman citizenship.)

The feeling that the Ottoman Empire had transformed from absolutist rule into a quasi-liberal parliamentary democracy triggered lofty expectations of Jewish civic integration. Unlike the European nation-states, where integration and civil equality were regarded ambivalently, and were premised on shedding communal identities, the post-1908 Ottoman regime was regarded as pluralistic, allowing Jews, Greeks, Armenians and Turks, and Arabs alike to breathe the same fresh air of freedom while keeping communal autonomy. The call of "Jews, become Ottomans!" was promoted in the family's newspapers, and Ben-Avi's memoir, despite being written years later, did not conceal his excitement at meeting Mustafa Kemal Atatürk in 1911. In 1914, with the outbreak of World War I, he toyed with enlisting in the Ottoman army. His audacious – though futile – attempt to Latinise the Hebrew alphabet was also inspired by the Turks, who introduced the *Türk alfabesi*, a new 29-letter Latin-script Turkish alphabet.

However, Ben-Avi's admiration for Atatürk cooled after the family's newspaper was closed by the Ottoman authorities in 1915. Though no official reason was given, Ben-Avi admitted that the paper was sympathetic to France and Britain, and the family temporarily relocated to the United States. When Palestine switched hands and was occupied by the British, Ben-Avi and his father adapted to the radically new political circumstances with the same zeal that Ottomanisation had inspired. They regarded the Balfour Declaration as the dawn of a new age, going as far as to suggest that the Zionists should create their own calendar, considering "Balfour Day" (2 November 1917) as year zero, from which the counting of time should commence – a Jewish nationalist tribute to the French revolutionary *calendrier républicain*. Even his journalistic style became more English: wishing to replicate the commercial success of Lord Northcliffe's *Daily Mail* – notorious for its hyperbolic style and unabashed promotion of jingoistic imperialist politics – in 1919 Ben-Avi founded the daily *Doar Hayom* (*Daily Mail*), which quickly acquired a similarly questionable reputation. Respectability was not his prime concern. The newspaper was designed to whet readers' appetites for sensational stories, to provide quick answers to complicated problems and to serve Ben-Avi's penchant for the epic and melodramatic. Asked to compare his newspaper to *Haaretz*, the reputable competitor known for the quality of its writers (also established in 1919), Ben-Avi reportedly quipped, "*Haaretz* may be a decent newspaper, but it is not a newspaper; *Doar Hayom* may not be decent, but it is a newspaper!" Perhaps.

More than reporting about local and world events, *Doar Hayom* provided Ben-Avi with a platform to promote his own, often idiosyncratic visions for the future of the region. Early on, he promoted what came to be known as the "Cantonisation plan": the division of Palestine into separate autonomous zones for Muslims, Christians and Jews, modelled after the Swiss Confederation. Canton Judea, the Jewish district he envisioned, was not centred around Jerusalem but stretched along the shores of the Mediterranean, consisting of Tel Aviv and Netanya, a city 30 kilometres north of Tel Aviv that he helped found in 1928. The plan was compared to the Irish Free State (which was still, at that stage, a dominion state that had not seceded from the British Commonwealth and whose citizens were expected to declare their fidelity to the British crown) and described as the most pragmatic solution to settle Arab–Jewish strife. Ben-Avi even went so far as to offer an accompanying interpretation

DEROR

(LIBERTY)

an illustrated hebrew weekly in latin characters

Shevudn ivri metzuyar ba katav ha ivri ha qadmon, ha-lo hen ha otyot ha latiniyot

ha órékh: ITTAMAR BEN-AVI

MEHHIR HA MENIYA

be Eretz-Yisrael
le shana 75 gerush
le hhatzi shana 40 gerush

mi hhutz le artzénu
le shana 1.25 gerush
le hhatzi shana 65 gerush

sarhhoq (Tel.) 272, Tel-Aviv

MEHHIR HA MODAÒT

be âmmud rishon
Kol inch qatann 5 gerush

bi shear âmmudim
Kol inch qatann 3 gerush

LE MODAÒT SHENATIYOT MEHHIRIM MEYUHHADIM

ha mian: Maárékhet "Deror"
44 Rehhov ha Sharon, Tel-Aviv

Kérekh I — (ha gillayon ba aretz 10 mil) — TEL-AVIV, Yomwaw, êrev Kislew 5694 (17 Nov. 1933) — (mi hhutz-la-àretz 20 mil) — Mispar 1

MA ÁNU ROTZIM?
ki sefat kenâan tihyé le qinyan kol yisrael we kol ha tevel
ÂSAROT MILIONIM YIQRE'U GAM YILMEDU ÎVRIT BI MEHIRUT

Lifné 10000 Shana
Amerika — Emm ha Tarbut!
KO MAKHRIZ PROFESSOR HENSELING

ÂL RÉGEL AHHAT
be ivrit latinit mevatteim kol ot we ot
A, E, I, O, U — niqraot kemo be latinit

SAKH-KOL MEHUMOT YÁFO
29 Harugim, 190 Petzuîm

Qenu ÎVRIT!

Bimeqom "Whisky and Soda"
Sheku "Carmel we Soda"
taim yoter, gam zol yoter

WE ARTZÉNU NEHENET

PHOENIX
Ba shavûa Ha ba

SHAÂRURIYA BE DIROT TEL-AVIV
ALFÉ ÓLIM MITGALGELIM BI REHHOVOTÉHA

ITTAMAR BEN-AVI

Ben-Avi's *Deror* (*Liberty*), a newspaper that used Latinised script for the Hebrew alphabet, 1933 of the Old Testament, arguing that the ancient Israelites were a talented and audacious seafaring people, and thus the Judean canton would provide a unique opportunity to restore Jews to the sea and to "re-Hebraise" the Mediterranean.

Outlandish as these ideas may appear to us, they did not fall on deaf ears. The Palestinian-Arab intellectual Ahmed Saleh Al-Khalidi was open to the possibility of converting Palestine into an Arab-Jewish confederation and proposed in 1934 that Jerusalem, Hebron, Safad, Nazareth and Bethlehem would be declared "neutral and holy" cities, with the latter two being attached to the Arab canton. British administrators such as L.G. Archer Cust and D.G. Harris also followed these discussions, and came up with their own preliminary "redistricting" plans, which ultimately provided a basis for the 1937 and 1947 partition plans.

In this fleeting "confederal" moment of transition between empires, the word *atzmaut* was born. The standard translation of *atzmaut* as "independence" – a political state of being separate, sovereign and divorced from a broader conglomerate – is, in fact, a mistranslation. Since there was already a Hebrew word indicating dependency (*tlut*), there was no need to coin a new term to describe the *lack* of dependence, a state of *i-tlut*. As Ben-Avi explained in his memoir, *atzmaut* was coined when he was searching for a modern Hebrew word for *autonomy*: a political condition of self-governance, not in isolation but within a broader entity such as a federation, commonwealth or empire. It was a nationalist daydream, centred around notions of developing autonomous Jewish life that would contribute to a culture of coexistence, rich with ethnic and religious diversity. "Here I saw in my imagination the 'end of days,' the vision of Isaiah," Ben-Avi wrote with characteristic pathos:

Here, the God of our ancestors sends before us the will and the courage to establish on their foundation the *atzmaut* (even then I created this word for the foreign word "autonomia") in all its glory. Like the Armenians, the Syrians, the Lebanese, the Albanians, the Yemenites, the Arabs.

We are accustomed to reading the history of Zionism as predicated on the idea of a Jewish nation-state. Conventional narratives insist on drawing a direct line between Theodor Herzl and the first Zionist Congress of 1897 and David Ben-Gurion declaring Independence in May 1948. Yet many of the thinkers and leaders of the Zionist movement did not aspire to establish a Jewish nation-state. As nationals or citizens of multinational empires, they perceived themselves as members of a minority in need of protection from the rule of the majority. It was not the idea of sovereignty that captured their imagination, but rather political models that restrained sovereignty and granted autonomy to various national groups.

Ben-Avi's lifetime coincided with a period of fundamental change – a transition between empires, world wars, an increase in ethnonational antagonism. A scandalous and turbulent personality, his political vision and the way he understood the word *atzmaut* cannot be separated from his hyperbolic writing style. Much of the reason he was not taken seriously had to do with the type of journalism he perfected: avoiding the humdrum and privileging oversimplified plots over narratives of nuance and complexity. His autobiography was a means to cast himself as a romantic, almost epic hero on a continuous quest, always on the move, constantly facing trials and adversaries. He called himself the Jerusalemite and took pride in his public persona as the first Hebrew child, but he immigrated to America after failing to find a livelihood in

Palestine. He died in New York in 1943 (almost two decades before the publication of his autobiography). With the Israeli Declaration of Independence, five years later, the word he coined was hijacked and acquired new meaning. But revisiting him invites us to re-evaluate this forgotten history of non-statist Zionist thinking. ▤

My (Jewish) Martinique

William F.S. Miles

Lamentin, French West Indies

In the open-air rotunda, as per West Indian custom and French administrative law, a plate of glass covers the top of the casket so that well-wishers from across the island can pay their last respects to the *grande dame* in her final repose. Religious images surrounding the body are classic Catholic: cross, Virgin Mary, etc. For some, the deceased – embalmed and decked out in her finest white dress – exhibits the accumulated beauty of her ninety-one years; for others, criticism of the embalmers' work is severe. The woman's eldest daughter, of the latter camp, is crying from both revulsion at the exposed body and the pain of losing a parent.

When I first came to Martinique on a Fulbright–French Government Teaching Assistantship forty-one years ago, this was the kind of deep and intense exposure to the local culture that I craved. But I have long since crossed the line from observing to participating in Martinican life. For the body in the casket is that of my loving mother-in-law; the sobbing daughter is my wife, mother of our two hybrid Franco-Martinico-American Jewish children.

The next day, for the funeral, I sit in Notre Dame de la Nativité, the Catholic church on Rue de Madiana in the village centre of

Schoelcher. I am one of very few white people in the church. I am certainly the only one there who, when my mother-in-law's soul is being blessed in Latin, dons a kippah and recites the Kaddish. I wonder if it is the first time, since the consecration of the church in 1888, that Hebrew has been uttered under its arches.

During my first academic year in Martinique in 1981, I did not meet a single Jew. But when I returned the following year, at the approach of Yom Kippur I used the pre-internet method of scouting out fellow Hebes: looking up Cohens and Levis in the phonebook. One phone Cohen led to another *Juif* until I'd met an airplane pilot named Jean Cohen and a jeweller named Elie Illouz. The latter directed me to the synagogue – a rented building near the national archives – where he himself led services. It wasn't until an electrical blackout during the Kol Nidre service that I realised Elie knew the once-a-year liturgy by heart. There were dozens of fellow worshippers – all male, as per Orthodox custom – intoning cadences very unfamiliar to this descendant of Polish and Lithuanian Jews. In fact, when I first heard *tefillot* (prayers) in the Sephardi synagogue, I thought I had entered a mosque. They prayed here like they had been doing so for centuries. But these were spiritual, not genealogical, descendants of earlier Martinican Jews.

The first Jews to live on this French island in the Caribbean were Dutch refugees, expelled from Brazil by the Portuguese. They arrived in 1654, only to be expelled in 1685 by Louis XIV. Waivers in the eighteenth century allowed individual Jews to resettle, on condition that they not outwardly practise their Judaism; such enforced assimilation meant that within a few generations, they had "become white" like the colonists. While individual Jews made their way to Martinique from metropolitan France in the nineteenth and early twentieth centuries, there was no Jewish community as such. Only after France abdicated to Nazi Germany in 1940 were the two dozen Jewish adults and their children living on the island forced into a virtual collectivity: a "Jews list" compiled by the gendarmerie. Other Jews, along with non-Jewish intelligentsia and anti-fascists, were detained in a former Martinican leper colony after leaving France and stopping on the island in transit. As of 2021, three former hidden Jewish children of occupied France were still living in Martinique: Arlette Cohen-Rosa, who became a photographer-journalist for the French Communist Party; Fanny Auguiac, orphaned by Nazi concentration camps, who for thirty-three years directed the island's cultural services; and André Thalmann, agro-industrialist, specialist in the processing of pineapple products.

As late as the 1970s, Martinique was still perceived as a kind of Wild West for young, ambitious, entrepreneurial Frenchmen who felt stifled in Old France. This included those North African (Sephardic) Jews who had fled Algeria, Tunisia and Morocco for France when their governments turned increasingly hostile following Israel's independence in 1948, and then again after the 1967 Six-Day War. Some of those ventured to Martinique to seek their fortune or because they had adapted poorly to the cultural and meteorological climes of the Metropole. These were the Sephardim with whom I prayed on that Yom Kippur back in 1982.

Today, that Sephardic community remains close-knit and vibrant. I have observed, interviewed and *davened* to the hilt in Martinique. My children attended summer camp at the *Kenaf ha'Aretz* (Ends of the Earth) synagogue; my son studied there for his bar mitzvah with an irascible and chain-smoking rabbi of mysterious origins and dubious financial concerns. I have had festive meals with the British-headed Chabad family sent to minister to the Francophone island Jews. One of my closest friends from Martinique is a French Jewish neurologist of Tunisian origin. My Martinique identity as academic and Ashkenazi vies with that of husband and in-law: the American Jewish member of a nominally Catholic French West Indian family, one of whose members – my wife – formally converted. Through these two sets of lenses I apprehend Martinique.

*

Twice I interviewed the late Aimé Césaire, co-founder of Négritude, the French Black consciousness movement, a kind of French precursor to Black Lives Matter. Césaire was born in 1913 on the grounds of a Martinican plantation, Eyma in Basse Pointe, owned in the eighteenth century by Jewish brothers David and Moïse Gradis. Césaire was well aware of this Jewish connection to his birthplace.

The first time we met, Césaire and I spoke about Martinican politics; the second, about French and West Indian Jewishnesss. I broached the Jewish question by asking him about a tree.

"You spoke about it on a radio program two weeks ago," I began. "A caller asked you about a tree locally called 'ear of Negro, ear of Jew'."

"Ear of mulatto," the ageing icon corrected me. He began sketching on a sheet of paper. "Look," he said, showing me. "The fruit of the tree, when dried, looks like a human ear. It could be the ear of a Black man, or the ear of a Jew. We could call the tree 'ear of a human being', for all it matters." He wrote, in Latin, the tree's botanical name.

"The reason I bring this up," I said, "is that, having researched former French colonies over these many years, I have now come to work on my own culture and patrimony – Jewish."

Surprise flashed across the face of the poet-professor-playwright-statesman. His secretary too.

"*Formidable!*" he said in a tone of congratulation.

I held back from replying *merci*. "So I have come to ask what place the Jew occupies in Martinican, in French West Indian, consciousness."

At first, Césaire shrugged. But then, animated, he was transported back in his mind to his arrival, as a teenager, at the Lycée Louis-le-Grand, in Paris in the 1930s.

"Up to that point, all I knew was that there were whites and blacks. I didn't know that there was this subdivision, Jew." He recalled the names of long-departed friends, teachers and acquaintances whom he knew from his Paris *lycée* before World War II.

"My schoolmates talked about the most brilliant professors at our great *lycée*. There was a great Latinist – Bloch. And a Hellenist – Jacqueline David. She was very pretty, by the way – very black hair, somewhat brown in complexion. She looked a bit Spanish to me, even reminded me of some of our own West Indian women … She did her thesis on Thucydides, married a man of French nobility." Césaire mentioned her admittance to the French Academy. (She was the second woman so honoured.)

"And then I discovered that they, along with the other most brilliant teachers we had, were Jewish." Some classmates would point them out – disparagingly, he said. "'This one is a Jew, that one is a Jew.' From that, I concluded that the Jews were the most intelligent ones around … So it was in France that I first heard about Jews, as a group set apart somewhat. But in Martinique, nobody talked about Jews."

Césaire changed that. In *Return to My Native Land*, his pathbreaking 1947 poetic declaration of Black consciousness in the French-speaking world, he wrote of:

the famine-man, the insult-man, the torture-man …
one can at any moment seize, beat up or kill – yes really kill him –
without having to account to anybody,
without having to excuse oneself to anyone.
a jew-man,
a pogrom-man
a little tyke,
a bum

And what is the solution, in *Return to My Native Land*, to the alienation, helplessness and statelessness of the French West Indian?

To leave.
As there are hyena-men and leopard-men,
    I would be a jew-man …

This passage was on prominent display in an exhibit on Césaire produced by UNESCO that toured in Paris, Dakar and Martinique in 1998. The exhibit's catalogue was more explicit:

The Negro is also the Jew, the foreigner, the Amerindian,
the illiterate, the untouchable, he who is different, the neighbor;
in brief, he who, by his very existence, is threatened, excluded,
marginalized, forgotten, sacrificed.

On 17 April 2008, Aimé Césaire died in Martinique.
Long before – in Paris, in the middle of July 1942 – 13,000 Jews were rounded up and herded into a bicycle racing stadium. From there, they were transported by train to their fates in Auschwitz.

Beginning in 1995, France has observed a national day of memorial every 16 July.

That commemoration extends to Martinique – a name that, for so many, is synonymous with tropical paradise. Twice I have stood alongside my mostly Sephardic co-religionists as the representative of the French government, the prefect, lays a wreath and recalls the darkest episode in France's Nazi-occupied past. The first time was at the solemn War Memorial on the capital's leafy Savannah, overlooking Fort-de-France Bay. The second was outside Saint Antoine-de-Padoue Church in the capital's gritty Terres Sainville neighbourhood. An embarrassing, tragi-comic scene unfolded, as the dignified prefect in starched white naval uniform was visibly unnerved by an intoxicated local vagabond muttering incoherently and pacing just metres away.

After forty years of intimate familiarity, Martinique has come to conjure more complex, and often sombre, associations than "field site" and "research topic". Here I have reckoned with mortality – that of in-laws, of mentors, of friends. Jews have been present throughout the island's modern history – in the background, yes, but acknowledged on occasion. The beauty of the island, combined with memories of antisemitism, haunt me in their paradox. It is a postlapsarian, postcolonial Eden where I have found love and loss, *négritude* and *neshuma*, Jewry and Humanity. This is my (Jewish) Martinique. ≡

The Ukraine pogroms: Genesis of a genocide

Mark Glanville

In the Midst of Civilized Europe: The Pogroms of 1918–1921 and the Onset of the Holocaust
Jeffrey Veidlinger
Metropolitan Books (US)/Picador (UK)

The title of Jeffrey Veidlinger's important and timely new book, *In the Midst of Civilized Europe*, is taken from an October 1919 letter to which the French journalist, writer and poet Anatole France was the lead signatory: "In the very midst of civilized Europe," runs the letter, "… the existence of a whole population is threatened. Such crimes dishonour not only the people that commit them, but outrage human reason and conscience." Much of Veidlinger's book is based on original research into eyewitness accounts preserved in the memorial books of the YIVO archive and other contemporary chronicles. Veidlinger writes that he "had always thought that the Holocaust was simply inconceivable before it happened", but his account of the Ukrainian pogroms in the period immediately following the Great War shows it to be not only conceivable but anticipated by contemporary Cassandras, even if none correctly guessed who its executioners would turn out to be. 'MASS MEETING HEARS THAT 127,000 JEWS HAVE BEEN

KILLED AND 6,000,000 ARE IN PERIL,' screamed a breath-takingly prophetic *New York Times* headline in 1919.

Little in Veidlinger's book suggests that Ukraine in the first half of the twentieth century would match most people's definition of the term "civilised". When so-called civilisation does intrude, it is in the shape of White Army officers, "pogrom-mongers with university diplomas in their hands, with noble titles, with French words on their tongues", as the folklorist Shmuel Rubinshteyn observed. Between 1918 and 1921, pogroms in Ukraine led to the murder of 100,000 Jews, the flight of 600,000 Jewish refugees and the internal displacement of several million more. Throughout this period, Jews were perceived as the *fons et origo* of their gentile neighbours' woes, and a legitimate target for their violently expressed grievances. Twenty-one years later, the work of the local population was completed by the Nazis with the almost complete annihilation of Ukrainian Jewry, the death toll of 1.4 million representing close to a quarter of the total Jewish victims of the Holocaust. Most were murdered close to their homes, with neighbours offering assistance to the Nazis.

While the alarm about these pogroms was raised at the time, today they have been mainly forgotten, dwarfed by the much greater destruction of the Holocaust. As Veidlinger explains, "The Nazi German genocide, with its unprecedented scale and horrifying death toll, offered the prospect of a type of absolution, the opportunity to remove the evidence of past atrocities and to relativize the sins of the previous generation, to allow the pogroms to be forgotten amid far greater villainy."

During the period under consideration, Ukraine was the centre of violent conflict between Ukrainian nationalist groups such as the Central Rada (modelled, paradoxically, on the Soviets), the

Bolshevik Red Army intent on spreading the revolution, and Poles struggling to establish a Polish nation-state. All projected the traits of their enemies onto Ukrainian Jews. To the Bolsheviks, Jews were bourgeois nationalists, to Ukrainian nationalists they were Bolsheviks, and to many Poles they were aliens and enemies of the new Polish republic.

But it was hatred of Bolshevism and "the perceived pre-eminence of Jews in that movement" that Veidlinger, in step with recent scholarship, locates as the driving force behind the massacres, both during the Holocaust and in the earlier pogroms that are the book's subject. Jews did, of course, play an important role in the Bolshevik movement. A former Talmud student and Cheka death squad leader, Yakov Yurovsky, murdered Tsar Nicholas II and his family in Ekaterinburg, while the Bolsheviks' most visible representative was Lev Davidovich Bronstein, better known as Trotsky, whose Jewish origins seem to have escaped the author of a bizarre 1917 graffito that proclaimed: "DOWN WITH THE JEW KERENSKY! LONG LIVE TROTSKY!" (Alexander Kerensky, leader of the Russian Republic overthrown by the Bolsheviks, was, unlike Trotsky, a gentile.) The anti-Soviet forces, both Ukrainian and Russian, that terrorised the towns and villages of Ukraine during this period laboured under no such illusions. Instead, they went out of their way to ensure that the local population knew who the enemy was. Antisemitism was a useful tool. As Veidlinger makes clear, "The military had difficulty motivating peasants to fight against an abstract idea like Bolshevism but was easily able to muster recruits when the Jews were presented as the threat." The Bolsheviks, meanwhile, identified antisemitism as a hallmark of the enemy. After the particularly savage Cherkasy pogrom, a headline in the Soviet Communist Party newspaper *Pravda* ran,

"TO BE AGAINST THE JEW IS TO BE FOR THE TSAR." Nikolai Ezhov, who as head of the NKVD (forerunner to the KGB, now the FSB) went on to purge many Jewish personnel, remarked, "When I went to Ukraine, they told me that many Jews worked there. But they deceived me – only Jews worked there." Veidlinger points out that, "In October 1921, about 10% of the nearly 50,000 employees of the Cheka across Soviet territories had Jewish backgrounds, even though Jews made up less than 2% of the overall population." The historian Leonard Schapiro noted in 1961 that "anyone who had the misfortune to fall into the hands of the Cheka stood a very good chance of finding himself confronted with and possibly shot by a Jewish investigator".

While some Jews thrived under Communism, and did indeed become the movement's assassins, most Jews were just as much victims of the Bolsheviks as their gentile neighbours. The Bolshevik ban on private enterprise and the nationalisation of industry had ruinous effects on Jewish artisans. And unfounded accusations of being a Bolshevik were often simply pretexts for looting wealthy, middle-class Jews. An example was the Zhytomyr pogrom, in which "the worst of the violence was directed against the wealthy bourgeoisie – the segment of the population least likely to be sympathetic to Bolshevism".

Chillingly, in the savage Proskuriv pogrom that ensued soon after, the troops' commander, Ivan Semosenko, asked that there be no repeat of the Zhytomyr pogrom, "during which the reputation of the Ukrainian army was sullied by looting and theft". Instead, Semosenko encouraged an assault on all Jews as Bolsheviks. "Everybody is saying that my Cossacks slaughtered peaceful residents, women, and children. This is nonsense!" declared Semosenko. "According to my orders, they only fought Bolsheviks. I gave a command to root out Bolsheviks. If Jewish women, children, and the elderly are Bolsheviks, it is their fault, not mine." The book contains a harrowing photograph of the corpses of some of his victims. One of them is a naked baby girl.

Against the backdrop of a war with the Bolsheviks that had spread from Russia to Ukraine hot on the heels of World War I, and the subsequent Polish–Soviet War of 1920, a generation had emerged that was "inured … to barbarism and brutality", argues Veidlinger. But one wonders how much encouragement was needed to harness the region's latent violent antisemitism – even if, as Veidlinger asserts, the previous generation had enjoyed better relations with Jewish neighbours. The unbridled savagery of these pogroms, involving rape, mutilation and dehumanising rituals – including forced dancing, an old form of antisemitic humiliation that can be found in the Brothers Grimm – points to a much deeper hatred of Jews that can arguably be traced back at least as far as the 1648 uprisings led by Hetman Bodhan Khmelnytskyi and the savage attacks on the Jewish communities that followed. Proskuriv, site of a particularly brutal pogrom in 1919, has since been renamed Khmelnytskyi, in what Veidlinger terms, somewhat kindly, an irony of history. Such a renaming certainly might suggest a sentimental attachment to Khmelnytskyi and his Cossack hordes, idolised by Ukrainian Christians as much as they were cursed and lamented by Jews.

Symon Petliura, who played such a significant role in the events detailed in this book before being assassinated in Paris in 1926 by Sholem Schwarzbard, certainly understood this. Exploiting the largely mythical idea that modern-day Ukrainians were descendants of the Cossacks who had terrorised Jewish communities 250 years earlier, he dressed his peasant units in the "papakha"

Astrakhan hat of the Cossacks and named his military units after Cossack bands and heroes, even adopting the Cossack title Otaman for himself and calling his soldiers Haidamaks. Yet the Central Rada he represented had started out as an inclusive organisation, expanding from 150 to 800 seats, nearly a third of which went to national minorities in an attempt "to reflect the genuinely tolerant ethos of the Ukrainian socialist leadership". The Central Rada even introduced banknotes with inscriptions not only in Ukrainian, Russian and Polish but also in Yiddish, and young Jews established brigades they hoped Petliura would include as regiments in his army.

Petliura, who emerges in Veidlinger's book as an ambiguous figure, had little control over the frequently antisemitic warlords who fought in his name. One of these was Ilya Struk. "We have a common enemy: the enemy is the Jew who wants to take all of our wealth" and "Long live our national character" were among Struk's slogans. Struk then switched sides, his band becoming the 20th Soviet Regiment of the Ukrainian front. He wore "a sailor's uniform, with a red star on his chest and the military service cap, waving a red banner with the words, 'Death to the bourgeoisie' and 'Long Live Soviet Power'". His antisemitic rhetoric also shifted. Instead of being Bolsheviks, Jews were now capitalists. In one proclamation, he confusingly refers to "Communist-Capitalist Jews". As Veidlinger notes, "Whether he was claiming allegiance to the Ukrainian People's Republic, the Bolsheviks, or the Whites, his antipathy toward the Jews remained constant. To many of those who followed him, this was really all that mattered."

Another figure swift to switch allegiances in mercenary fashion was Nikifor Grigoriev, who termed his former Bolshevik allies Christ-killers and bloodsuckers, plastering manifestos on the walls of towns he occupied with slogans such as "Instead of land and freedom, they have forcefully imposed upon you a commune, special police, and commissars from the Moscow gluttons and the lands where they crucify Christ". "Rousing anti-Jewish hatred," writes Veidlinger, "was Grigoriev's most potent weapon."

Neither Petliura, with his declarations of freedom, nor the Bolsheviks, with their promise of land redistribution, were able to make good on their promises. "In the absence of any political ideology to believe in," says Veidlinger, "many became susceptible to the conspiracy theory that the Jews were to blame for all their problems." Much of what motivated the players in this sorry story seems to have been simple opportunism. Communism, nationalism, even antisemitism, were useful rallying cries, not always underpinned by deeply held convictions.

Older forms of antisemitism also contributed to the mix, as in Slovechno. There, a pogrom was triggered by concerns that the Bolsheviks were intending to transfer ownership of the register of births, deaths and marriages from the priest to the Soviet executive committee. "It was often the Bolsheviks' attacks on the church that most antagonized the masses, and that contributed to the popular association between Jews and Bolsheviks: many pious Christians could not imagine one of their own profaning the church," writes Veidlinger. And when a pogrom occurred, the peasants shouted the slogan of the tsarist Black Hundreds: "Hurrah! Beat the Yids!" Ukrainian antisemites, like the antisemites of today, happily invoked past tropes and slogans to furnish their contemporary version of the virus of antisemitism.

Veidlinger's book comes out at a time when Ukraine has become, once again, a victim of its eastern neighbour's aggression, and most now would rather not be reflecting on the events it details – events President Putin has been exploiting, cynically and dishonestly, to discredit the modern state. Volodymyr Zelensky, Ukraine's Jewish president, is living evidence of the extent to which his country has indeed become civilised since the events outlined in the book: Ukraine emerged from a recent pre-invasion poll as the least antisemitic nation in Eastern Europe. But even Zelensky has chosen to gloss over that part of his country's history: "Zelensky asked the 'people of Israel' to make a choice, just as Ukrainians made their choice eighty years ago," Veidlinger wrote in a recent article.

> With 2,673 Ukrainians recognized by Yad Vashem for their efforts to save Jews, Zelensky can legitimately boast that "Righteous Among the Nations are among us," as he did in his speech [to the Knesset in March]. But this claim obscures the role that far more Ukrainians played in collaborating with the Germans and facilitating the murder of their Jewish neighbours.

One can understand why Zelensky and others would rather not recall that troubling period in their country's history at this juncture. But it would be better, surely, to celebrate the modern country's progress by acknowledging it and commemorating its victims as Veidlinger does, in this major contribution to the history of the pogrom in the early twentieth century. ≡

The Sassoon dynasty: Worldly Jews in a globalised world

Sarah Abrevaya Stein

The Global Merchants: The Enterprise and Extravagance of the Sassoon Dynasty
Joseph Sassoon
Allen Lane

The extraordinary story of the Sassoon family has been told by many, and viewed in many different lights: they were commanders of vast investments, fortunes and supply chains; pioneers of a global, mercantile, familial diaspora that stretched from eighteenth-century Ottoman Mesopotamia to South and South-East Asia, England, across the British Commonwealth and beyond.

In 1941, the prodigious Anglo-Jewish historian Cecil Roth introduced English-language readers to the Sassoon family as a model of Jewish-British imperial symbiosis. There was greatness in the family, as Roth saw it, but also greatness in an empire that allowed the grandson of a Baghdadi-born, eighteenth-century Jewish family patriarch to emerge (along with the likes of Wilfred Owen, Rupert Brooke and Robert Graves) as a bard of the Great War – Siegfried Sassoon (1886–1967), grandson of David Sassoon (1792–1864). Though Roth didn't acknowledge it, Siegfried was also a closeted gay man, haunted by the black dog, who died the year homosexuality was finally legalised in Britain. It is a stunning reminder of how time, in the history of the Sassoon family, has an accordion-like quality, compressing and stretching to accommodate the astonishing restrictions and expansions of modern history.

Other writers followed in Roth's wake. Joan Roland, author of the pathbreaking *Jews in British India: Identity in a Colonial Era* (1989), saw the Sassoon family in their South Asian incarnation as representing one powerful pole that rooted Jewish life in a nineteenth-century colonial India defined by imbalances of race, class and power, where wealthy Jews of Ottoman Mesopotamian origin existed on one side of a racialised class binary. (The Bene Israel, the native community of western India – poorer, browner and with a religious tradition the immigrant Baghdadi Jews looked down upon – occupied the other.) Maisie J. Meyer, in *From the Rivers of Babylon to the Whangpoo: A Century of Sephardi Jewish Life in Shanghai* (2003), and Chiara Betta, in a series of articles, stepped forward to claim the Sassoons and the wider Baghdadi Jewish diaspora as colourful actors in the multi-ethnic, multi-sectarian, multi-layered treaty port city of nineteenth- and twentieth-century Shanghai. A similar, even more florid take was adopted by Jonathan Kaufman in this year's *The Last Kings of Shanghai*, whose subtitle frames the Sassoons as one of "the rival Jewish dynasties that helped create modern China". (The other was the Kadoorie family.)

In 2016, I joined this modest scrum. My book, *Extraterritorial Dreams: European Citizenship, Sephardi Jews, and the Ottoman Twentieth Century*, situates the generation of young, Ottoman-born Jewish merchants and their families who followed the Sassoons to South and South-East Asia as legal problems for British bureaucrats. Over the first half of the twentieth century, Britain struggled to legally define these "extraterritorial" subjects of a now-defunct

Ottoman Empire, to which they had once made promises of legal reciprocity. It wasn't just an abstract question: vast fortunes and estate taxes hung in the balance.

Each of these efforts to grapple with the Sassoons and their various legacies has its strengths, but all suffer from the same pitfall: they have segmented one aspect or geography of the Sassoon family's history at the expense of a broader view. Sources have played a role in this tunnel vision. Until now, no scholar has had the access (or, no less significantly, the linguistic range) required to explore the Sassoon family archive, a rich repository of thousands of documents dating from 1855 to 1949, much of which was written in Baghdadi-Jewish dialect to keep documents of commercial exchange from the prying eyes of competitors. These materials, acquired by the National Library in Jerusalem, have only recently been catalogued and made available to scholars.

At last, with Joseph Sassoon's *The Global Merchants*, we are blessed with an alternative, expansive approach, telling the history of the Sassoons as participants in the global economy and citizens of the modern world. "Their story is," Sassoon writes in the introduction,

> not just that of an Arab-Jewish family who settled in India, traded in China and aspired to be British, but also a vista to the world in which they lived and prospered as well as its major developments – from the American Civil War to the opium wars, the opening of the Suez Canal and introduction of the telegraph, as well as the mechanisation of textile production. The era they inhabited was driven above all by an encompassing globalisation, which they and other merchants benefitted from and influenced, and which shaped our world today.

The Global Merchants is a brilliant work, and long overdue. How touching that it comes from a scholar related to the extended family in question, though distantly.

Joseph Sassoon's story begins in Ottoman Mesopotamia, a static backdrop to most previous accounts of the Sassoons' history but engagingly handled in *The Global Merchants*. The family patriarch with whom he begins is Sheikh Sassoon ben Saleh Sassoon, appointed in 1781 as chief treasurer of the Sultan (and consequently lay head of the Baghdadi Jewish community), only to find himself in the disfavour of the province's new and irascible governor. The governor, who had risen to power due in part to the Jewish community's support, squeezed Baghdad's Jews for money as his own debts to Constantinople rose. In the chaotic and dangerous situation that ensued, Sheikh Sassoon sent his son David, heir to his father's financial know-how and fortune, to Bushir, a coastal city in Iran. Father soon followed. Their departure, sometime between 1828 and 1830, was fortuitous, for it kept them at a distance from a plague and flood that soon struck their native city. Sheikh Sassoon passed away in Bushir and David travelled on to Bombay.

His choice of Bombay was born of the skill set that would serve David and his descendants well for many years. Sheikh Sassoon's son was fluent in many languages (he learned Hindustani soon after arriving in Bombay, complementing his knowledge of Arabic, Hebrew, Turkish and Persian) and could rely for information and advice on the wide, multi-ethnic network of merchants with whom his family did business. Bombay was a city of opportunity – David realised this before leaving Bushir – and his contacts helped him establish himself quickly in his new home. With his vast and valuable assets – experience in business, linguistic dexterity, relationships of trust, established networks across regional boundaries – David began to build an empire.

As Joseph Sassoon notes, family was paramount. David was a talented businessman and a devoted father. He was also something of a micro-manager. With his first wife, Hannah, and second wife, Farha, he had six sons and four daughters. Thirty-nine years separated the birth of the first from that of the last. "Together," writes Sassoon, "they formed a little army." David was insistent that the boys' education was thorough, that they sought independence at an early age and that they recognised him and the family business as the hub of the family. Sassoon & Company (also known as David Sassoon & Sons) was born.

Sassoon & Company was trading primarily in cotton, tea and silk when Britain's triumph in the First Opium War (1839–1842) resulted in the rapacious Treaty of Nanking, which granted Britain authority over Hong Kong and five other ports along China's south-east coast. Foreign firms rushed to capitalise on the moment, and David, always attuned to opportunity, was determined that the Sassoon family be among them. He adopted a strategy of rotating his sons (especially Elias, Abdullah and Sassoon David, known as SD) between commercial entrepôts – especially Bombay, Shanghai, Hong Kong and London – crucial to the evolving global economy.

Following the Treaty of Nanking, opium was legalised in China, soon becoming the most valuable commodity imported to Shanghai. Along with tea, opium became the foundation of a wildly lucrative – though also exploitative – triangle trade between India, China and Britain, and Sassoon & Company were among those to profit. Yet, while tea and opium clinched the family's mercantile success story, their portfolio was cannily diversified. Sassoon quotes a colleague of the family on their ever-expanding reach: "Silver and gold, silks, gums, and spices, opium and cotton, wool and wheat – whatever moves over sea or land feels the hand or bears the mark of Sassoon & Co."

Communication was essential to the family's and the firm's success. Though they were early adopters of the telegraph, prior to that they had mastered the art of the letter, which they never abandoned. They were prodigious letter-writers in the many languages they spoke and wrote. Written communication, both epistolatory and by telegram, substantiated by personal and familial networks and that ever-important asset, trust, allowed the family to stay on top of, respond to and anticipate fluctuations in an unpredictable global market, caused by shifting views on the morality of the opium trade or the ebb and flow of the cotton trade brought about by the American Civil War.

Students of history might consider that Joseph Sassoon is to the Sassoon family what historian Sven Beckert (*Empire of Cotton: A Global History*, 2014) is to cotton – a meticulous researcher and talented storyteller seeking to weave the complex tale of a single subject into the weft of a large global tapestry. Both books are bound by the notion of political economy as a key to modern history. It is a compelling approach to the Sassoon story, with two pitfalls.

First, in contrast to Beckert, Joseph Sassoon pays relatively little heed to race or race capitalism – except when it comes to the lens of antisemitism, through which the British aristocracy persistently viewed the Sassoon family. This gap in Sassoon's account is striking. It deprives us of an opportunity to think about the broader implications of Jews' relationship to racial capitalism, of which they were a conduit.

Second, Sassoon's centring of political economy, so apt when the Sassoon family's fortunes were mighty, becomes something of a liability after the family's commercial disunion and fall from mercantile grace. An initial rupture in the Sassoon dynasty's commercial cohesion occurred after David's death when, in 1867, his son Elias broke off from David Sassoon & Co. to form E.D. Sassoon & Co., based in Shanghai. The remaining branches of the family firm carried on as Sassoon & Co., with Elias's brother Abdullah, based in Bombay, at its head. Both branches of the firm continued to thrive after the fissure and were dramatically bolstered by the opening of the Suez Canal, which radically decreased travel costs and time between Asia and Europe. Yet now the Sassoon family existed in internal competition, no longer as a single entity of global merchants.

Joseph Sassoon manages to keep many balls in the air while writing of the divergent – but still strong – branches of Sassoon & Co. As Elias solidified and enlarged his empire in Shanghai, Abdullah expanded David Sassoon & Co. in India and in his adopted home of London, where he became the toast of the city's aristocrats, anglicised his name to Albert and earned a knighthood. Meanwhile, Suleiman maintained control of operations in Bombay.

Sassoon brings together these different branches as he narrates the family's successful penetration of late-nineteenth and early-twentieth-century high society, at last drawing attention to the Sassoon women. Initially shadowy figures in *The Global Merchants*, now the Sassoon girls and women are central figures at fashionable balls and parties. One wishes their voices had come earlier, and were louder and less frivolous, but at least the course is modestly corrected.

Drawing a contrast with the frivolity of many of the women portrayed here, Joseph Sassoon digs deep into the history of Farha (née Abraham) Sassoon, the well-educated, perspicacious daughter of a prominent Jewish family from Bombay who married Suleiman and then took over the running of Sassoon & Co.'s Bombay branch after her husband's death. Remarkably, Farha ably managed all details of the business while mothering three young children. Then, just as her brothers-in-law sensed the possibility of another schism in both firm and family, Farha announced her retirement, though whether this was under pressure from the family or out of genuine volition is unclear.

The author dates the end of the era of the Sassoons as global merchants to the end of World War I, when David Sassoon & Co. "had lost its bearings and there was no obvious person within the Sassoons to take over the helm". The intensification of the anti-opium movement, which achieved its goals roughly by the end of World War I – far later than many wished, and not yet a complete victory – played a role, as did the war itself. But changes within the family had an impact too. Sassoon & Sons lacked direction, and after E.D. Sassoon passed from Elias to his son Jacob, Jacob found himself without a successor, or none who lasted in the position for long. "The innovation or vision that might have enabled the firm, now approaching its centenary, to survive and indeed thrive in a world that was changing rapidly was absent," writes Sassoon.

Around this point, *The Global Merchants* loses a bit of its drive too, giving the impression of dutiful summation rather than passionate engagement. Sassoon is less sure-footed as he tackles the waning decades of the family's prominence. He does not present himself as a genealogist or a cultural historian, and tying together the loosening threads of the dynasty's history is not his strong suit. By the last quarter of the book, it is not only the Sassoons who have lost something of their oomph, but their chronicler as well.

Nonetheless, *The Global Merchants* is an extraordinary achievement. Joseph Sassoon is judicious and successful in showing how the Sassoon history was shaped by – and shaped – global events and the ebbs and flows of the global economy. It is not the only way we might understand the family's story, but it is a crucial perspective, and one we have lacked until now. ▤

Hannah Arendt's portrait of an unhappy consciousness

Ryan Ruby

Rahel Varnhagen: The Life of a Jewish Woman
Hannah Arendt (trans. Clara Winston and
Richard Winston)
NYRB Classics

Born Rahel Levin in Berlin to a wealthy Jewish merchant one generation removed from the Breslau ghetto, Rahel Varnhagen (1771–1833) was a key figure connecting the German Enlightenment and Romanticism. As a young woman she ran a prominent salon in what was then the Prussian capital, during the last decade of the eighteenth century and the first decade of the nineteenth. On the top floor of her family's home on Jägerstraße she hosted members of the Hohenzollern court, including the composer-soldier Prince Louis Ferdinand, and intellectual luminaries such as the Humboldt brothers, Friedrich Schlegel, Friedrich Schleiermacher, Adelbert von Chamisso, Friedrich August Wolf and Jean Paul, among others. Never a great beauty and, after the death of her father, with no dowry to offer a prospective husband, she survived on her talents alone. Her broken engagements with diplomats Count Karl von Finckenstein and Don Raphael d'Urquijo were the talk of Berlin society; together with the nationalist turn taken after Napoleon's conquest of Prussia in 1806, they precipitated Rahel's fall from grace.

In 1808, Rahel met Karl August Varnhagen von Ense in Berlin, an unpromising medical student from the provinces fourteen years her junior, whose career as a civil servant and man of letters unexpectedly took off during the Wars of Liberation, in no small part thanks to her coaching. The last of her family to convert to Christianity, she married Karl in 1814. After nearly a decade travelling around Europe, including time in Paris, Vienna, Frankfurt and a three-year stint in Karlsruhe, the capital of the Grand Duchy of Baden, where Varnhagen served as the Prussian chargé d'affaires, the couple returned to Berlin for good in 1819. There, she became the friend and confidante of the young Heinrich Heine and renewed her salon activities, opening her home to the likes of novelist Bettina von Arnim, historian Leopold von Ranke and Hegel. Distant acquaintances of the author of *Faust*, she and her husband became the prime movers behind the so-called Goethe cult, a significant aspect of German culture and education to this day. Although she never wrote a book, the more than 6000 letters she left behind when she died of cholera in 1833 are an indispensable documentary source for the history and culture of the period.

Outside Germany, Rahel is perhaps best known as the subject of Hannah Arendt's *Habilitationsschrift*, the second dissertation after a doctoral thesis required to teach at a German university. It is not difficult to see what drew the 23-year-old Arendt to Rahel, whom she called "my closest friend, though she has been dead for some hundred years". In her recent biography, Samantha Rose Hill notes that Arendt was raised in a secular, middle-class Jewish household in Königsberg, where the educational philosophies of Goethe and Wilhelm von Humboldt, cultivated and promoted in Rahel's salons, were put into practice. Having discovered Rahel's life and correspondence through her childhood friend Anne Mendelssohn, a descendent of Moses Mendelssohn (whose daughters, Dorothea and Henriette, had been close friends of the young Rahel), Arendt began writing about Rahel in the aftermath of her affair with Heidegger, whose membership of the Nazi party and assumption of the rectorship at the University of Freiburg put the nail in the coffin of their doomed relationship. This is perhaps one reason why Rahel's own *amours fous* are so central to Arendt's account of her life.

While she was consulting the papers in the Varnhagen archive at the Prussian State Library on Unter den Linden, a short walk from Rahel's family home, Arendt was also engaged in dangerous clandestine research on behalf of the German Zionist Organization, documenting antisemitic statements published by the Nazi regime and distributing them abroad. It was not lost on Arendt that, one century after Rahel's death, the antisemitism that had delimited her legal and social status had become nothing less than the ruling principle of the German state, which was to have genocidal consequences that even she could not foresee. After an interrogation by the Gestapo in 1934, Arendt fled Germany with the first eleven chapters of the manuscript in her luggage, which she completed, at the behest of her friend Walter Benjamin, in exile in France in 1938. In 1940, having escaped on foot from the French internment camp of Gurs, she fled Europe with her second husband to the safety of New York; there, she would be responsible for transmitting the writings of Kafka, Benjamin and Gershom Scholem to new audiences, much as Rahel had done for Goethe and the habitués of her salons a century before. Except that the authors Arendt championed were Jewish, and doing so was not her raison d'être, but a sideline to her own career as one of the most important public intellectuals of the day.

Despite these affinities with her subject, in *Rahel Varnhagen: The Life of a Jewish Woman* – translated by Clara Winston and Richard Winston and published in 1958, following the tremendous successes of *The Origins of Totalitarianism* and *The Human Condition*, and now reissued by NYRB Classics – Arendt gives us what at first appears to be a cautionary tale rather than the story of an exemplary life. When it came out, readers expecting a conventional biography were disappointed. Reviewing the book, the English novelist Sybille Bedford described it as "a relentlessly abstract book – slow, static, curiously oppressive". Time has only confirmed this impression. Arendt takes for granted, rather than explaining, the importance of her principal character, and assumes a great degree of knowledge about the peripheral figures and historical context that even German readers might not have had. Important biographical details, such as the story of Rahel's visit to her Breslau family as a teenager, or her early meeting with Goethe, are left to the later chapters, and keen insights into, for example, the use of antisemitism as a wedge for a rising bourgeoisie to advance politically against the enlightened sectors of the Junker aristocracy, Prussia's landowning nobility, are sporadic. As a result, Arendt's forceful assertions about Rahel's character and personality often come across as over-generalised and under-earned.

In the preface, Arendt defends her departures from biographical conventions:

> It was never my intention to write a book about Rahel; about her personality … nor her position in Romanticism … nor about the significance of her salon … nor about her ideas … What interested me solely was to narrate the story of Rahel's life as she might have told it.

While Arendt stays very close to the documentary record – the book is a kind of philosophical dialogue with Rahel's (extensively quoted) correspondence – *Rahel Varnhagen* is not a simple narrativisation of the letters. Arendt's judgements intrude; and, in any case, the epistolary form is a kind of performance of the self whose interpretation requires some understanding of a letter's writer, its recipient and the local and broader circumstances that occasioned it. The picture that emerges from *Rahel Varnhagen* is less "Rahel's life as she might have told it" than a snapshot of Arendt's intellectual preoccupations at the time she wrote it. Which is all to the good, considering that is why, of course, we are reading it in the first place.

Rahel Varnhagen is a study in the lived experience of a structural contradiction. Rachel Levin, the individual, might have been born in Berlin at the end of the eighteenth century, but her history as a Jewish woman – and thus her "Destiny" and her "problem" – began "seventeen hundred years earlier in Jerusalem". Physically distanced from her ethnic and class origins by her father's financial success, she was thrust into a milieu in which she could not fully participate. As Arendt frames it, the complex and inescapable dialectic of "parvenu" (the desire to have a social identity from which one is excluded by birth) and "pariah" (the desire to be true to and even valorise one's identity as one of the excluded) would turn, to paraphrase her friend Hegel, into an "unhappy consciousness". We need not accept as authentic the words her husband claimed she uttered on her deathbed – "the thing which all my life seemed to me to be the greatest shame, which was the misery and misfortune of my life – having been born a Jewess" – to grant that in today's terms, Rahel would be called a "self-hating Jew". Her letters are full of such comments, which are uncomfortable to read. "I do not forget this shame for a *single* second," she was writing as late as

1810. "The Jew must be extirpated from us, that is the sacred truth, and it must be done even if life were uprooted in the process."

For Arendt, Rahel's error was that she took too seriously Enlightenment ideas about the autonomy of rational persons, Rousseau's sentimental confessionalism and the kind of self-fashioning portrayed by Goethe in *Wilhelm Meister*. What made Rahel equal, in her own view, to the "greatest artist, philosopher or poet" she hosted in her salons was that her "assigned task was *life*" – life lived as a work of art. Alas, in reading Goethe "as one reads the Bible", as she once advised a correspondent, Rahel did not realise that her idol was the exception that proved the rule: there is no happy overlap between one's individual personality, disposition and character and the position one is thrust into by historical circumstances beyond one's control. In Arendt's judgement, Rahel's attempt to "escape from Jewishness" as an individual, through "personal" rather than "political struggle", was condemned to fail from the outset.

Yet, the personal and political struggles inherent in Jewish identity do not map onto the notions of "assimilation" and "Zionism" as neatly as one might at first think. Writing in Berlin in the late 1920s or early 1930s, Arendt already understood that assimilation was no defence against antisemitism. Between then and the time she wrote the concluding chapters of *Rahel Varnhagen* in 1938, however, she had visited Palestine with Youth Aliyah, and seen the limitations of nation-state Zionism. Her first reaction to the kibbutzim, as she later told Mary McCarthy, was this: "I thought: a new aristocracy. I knew even then that one could not live there." In her published writings on the subject – from the journalism collected in *The Jewish Writings* to *Eichmann in Jerusalem* – she remained a consistent critic of Zionism. Her reasons are many, but in the prescient terms proposed in *Rahel Varnhagen*, it is that nation-states elevate the desires of the individual "parvenu" to the level of an entire people and, in doing so, create new "pariahs".

The contradiction between the parvenu and the pariah engenders four possible outcomes: segregation and extermination, Zionism, assimilation and individual pariahhood. The first was necessary to oppose without qualification, but of the remainder, individual pariahhood was the only one Arendt could bring herself to endorse. In the uproar following the publication of *Eichmann in Jerusalem*, she responded privately to the criticisms of her friend Gershom Scholem: "I'll begin with *ahavath Israel* … How right you are that I have no such love … I have never in my life 'loved' some nation or collective." In an open letter to Scholem published the following year in *Encounter* magazine, she added: "The trouble is that I am independent … I do not belong to any organization and always speak only for myself."

In this, too, Arendt had an antecedent in Rahel Varnhagen, and, fittingly, the last chapter of the biography shows a considerable softening towards her subject. She notes that despite Rahel's stated desire to "escape [her] Jewishness", she refused to convert on the occasions on which it would have been most advantageous to do so. Nor did she, like many recent converts, join the German patriotic fervour against Napoleon, even though this would have helped her repair her social standing. Even after her conversion and marriage to Varnhagen, Rahel maintained sympathy for those who had been cast out by society, such as her old friend Pauline, a former mistress of Prince Louis Ferdinand. The romantic individualism that deluded her into believing that she could be an equal member of German society through her talents alone prevented her, in the end, from relinquishing her uniqueness by assimilating. "Rahel had remained a Jew and a pariah," Arendt concludes.

"Only because she clung to both conditions did she find a place in the history of European humanity."

History's cruellest irony is that it gives each of us multiple identities and then creates conditions far too complex to allow us to choose any single one of them without painful contradiction. As the lives of both Rahel Varnhagen and Hannah Arendt attest, it is not the person who wholly embraces or wholly extirpates a given aspect of their identity that history most often remembers, but the person who cannot be reduced to any of them. ▤

Correspondence

*"After the Golden Age: American Jewish writing
in the twenty-first century" by Adam Kirsch*

Justin Cammy

Having just completed teaching a survey of American Jewish literature at a historically women's college, I am reminded that what was a "golden age" (for some overwhelmingly male writers and critics) is itself in need of interrogation. My students intelligently consumed the Roths (Henry and Philip) but were more intrigued by the saltiness of Grace Paley and the postmodern experimentation of biracial writer Fran Ross. And while they appreciated the moral seriousness of Bellow and the historical vision of E.L. Doctorow, they came alive when wrestling with early-twentieth-century modernist Yiddish poets and exploring the condition of living between languages and cultures offered by Achy Obejas in her queer Cuban American novel *Days of Awe*. Teaching Jewish American literature today is an exercise in rethinking seminal texts (no pun intended) and coming to terms with how canons are formed, and by whom.

It also was not lost on my students that American Jewish literature is no longer at the centre, and likely not even on the radar, of what is institutionally prioritised as American multicultural literature. When our English department recently changed one of its requirements from a course on ethnic American literature to one that encourages "the global/racial as a central category of analysis", the only literatures that are explicitly named are postcolonial, African American, Latinx and Native American. If Jewish American writers played a significant role in defining American literature in the second half of the twentieth century, they were barely included on syllabi by its end – too "white" for the new ethnic studies, and too Jewish to be taught alongside canonical American writers.

Adam Kirsch cites five mid-career writers as representatives of a recent turn in American Jewish letters that puts to rest Irving Howe's prophecy that American Jewish literature would write itself into oblivion because it had but a single story to tell – that of being "stamped and pounded by the immigrant experience". The socialist Howe could not imagine a generation of writers so secure in their Americanness that they would shift focus to their Jewishness. If Howe's imagined audience for Jewish writers was broadly American, today's Jewish writers seem to revel in "blowing into the narrow end of the shofar", as Cynthia Ozick encouraged in 1970. "If we chose mankind rather than Jewish and blow into the wider part," she warned, "we will not be heard at all." While I may quibble with Kirsch's choice of texts, he is ultimately correct in noting that what Ozick suggested has come to fruition: a Jewish American Republic of Letters that is centrally Jewish in its concerns. It should be emphasised that this turn, which began in the 1980s, was led by women – not only Ozick, but also Rebecca Goldstein, Allegra Goodman, Tova Mirvis and others who took Jewish life, and especially American Judaism, as a serious subject for literature.

Near the end of his essay, Kirsch gestures towards "other [new] strands and schools of Jewish literature [that] see Jewish life from distinctively different points of view". Here, Kirsch mentions writers who came to the United States just before or soon after the collapse of the Soviet Union. Kirsch might have paid them more attention. From Gary Shteyngart and David Bezmozgis to Lara Vapnyar, Anya Ulinich and Irina Reyn, we find an oft irreverent tone that overturns the former foundations of the Jewish immigrant novel by making biculturalism (rather than acculturation and even assimilation) the subject of fiction.

There are other strands, too, that Kirsch might have considered. First, the Jewish graphic novel. By now we know that Jewish artist-storytellers played a foundational role in the rise of American comics, a genre that reached new heights through the genius of Art Spiegelman (*Maus, In the Shadow of No Towers*) and Will Eisner. But a newer generation of graphic novelists is now worthy of attention. Consider *New Yorker* cartoonist Liana Finck, whose *A Bintel Brief* takes inspiration from a popular advice column in the early-twentieth-century Yiddish *Forverts* and guides readers through a history of Yiddish immigrant life. Similarly, Finck's just-released *Let There Be Light* offers a provocative feminist midrash on the Book of Genesis. (It is also worth mentioning J.T. Waldman, who produced one of the great literary interpretations of Esther in his graphic novel *Megillat Esther*.)

Second, more attention might be paid to works originally published in other languages and now appearing in translation. Here I might point to the recent burst in translation of works in Yiddish by women such as Chava Rosenfarb, Kadya Molodovsky, Blume Lempl, Miriam Karpilove and Fradl Shtok – each a revelation. Such translations significantly expand on what we understand American Jewish literature to have been. The same can be said of the Jewish Latin America Series edited by Ilan Stavans and published by the University of New Mexico Press in the late 1990s. It is not only that these texts bring Spanish- and Portuguese-language writers into broader consciousness, but that they open up a multilingual, hemispheric consideration of Jewish literature of the Americas that is no longer defined by the political borders of the United States.

Third, among the most exciting recent developments of Jewish literature is the degree to which it wrestles with previous Jewish texts. This deep inter-textual imagination is at the heart of Dara Horn's entire imaginative project, whether in *The World to Come*, which brings the Yiddish short story into the heart of contemporary American literature, or *All Other Nights*, whose interpretation of the Haggadah allows us to read Jews into both the Union and Confederate causes during the Civil War.

For my generation of students, the binary of Diaspora and Israel no longer holds. They prefer a model of multiple Jewish homelands, each of which offers something to the global Jewish cultural conversation. Here we might think of Ayelet Tsabari, a Yemini-Israeli who writes in English in Canada. Tsabari's collection of stories, *No Place Like Home*, and memoir, *The Art of Leaving*, not only centre Mizrahi experience and displace the Ashkenormativity of the American Jewish canon, but also offer a transnationalist perspective on the shifting meanings of the Jewish home. So long as twenty-first-century Jews continue reading and mining their cultural, linguistic and racial hybridity, they will be at home in the world.

Justin Cammy is a professor of Jewish studies and world literatures at Smith College. His critical edition of Abraham Sutzkever's From the Vilna Ghetto to Nuremberg: Memoir and Testimony *was a finalist for the 2021 National Jewish Book Award.*

David Brauner

Adam Kirsch's essay is characteristically eloquent and full of perceptive observations and enlightening readings of some of the key American Jewish fiction of the twenty-first century. However, in order to make his argument, he is strategically selective in his choice of authors and texts. He also makes some claims that are somewhat misleading. For example, he begins by asserting that the "the most exciting writers of the 1990s were the same ones who had presided over the golden age of Jewish fiction four decades earlier", identifying as his exemplary authors Philip Roth, Saul Bellow, Norman Mailer and Bernard Malamud. Yet, as Kirsch points out, Malamud had died in 1986; the fact that his posthumously published *Complete Stories* made the *New York Times* list of the best books of 1997 is hardly proof he was regarded as one "the most exciting writers of the 1990s". (The sad truth is that Malamud was largely forgotten by the end of the twentieth century and remains so, notwithstanding the heroic efforts of Philip Davis in his 2008 biography to rehabilitate his literary reputation.) Mailer's star was also very much on the wane in the 1990s; Kirsch's vague claim that Mailer's epic novel *Harlot's Ghost* "made the headlines" in 1991 does not disguise the fact that it was not generally well reviewed. (The telling detail here is that

Mailer anticipated writing a sequel but never did, discouraged by its luke-warm critical reception.) As for Bellow, well, yes – his final novel, *Ravelstein* (2000), represented a marked improvement on his only book of the 1990s (a mediocre 1997 novella entitled *The Actual*), but to call it a "triumph" is something of an overstatement.

In fact, of the four authors Kirsch cites as dominating the fictional landscape of the 1990s, only Philip Roth was really breaking new ground and enhancing his literary reputation: the other three were barely clinging to the margins of the canon. He also omits the exciting new work being produced in the 1990s by American Jewish writers in the medium of the short story – work that defies Kirsch's characterisation of this period as "the doldrums of late-twentieth-century Jewish writing". Rebecca Goldstein's collection *Strange Attractors* (1993) is an example, as are Amy Bloom's *Come to Me: Stories* (1993), Edith Pearlman's *Vaquita and Other Stories* (1996), Deborah Eisenberg's *All Around Atlantis* (1997) and Nathan Englander's *For the Relief of Unbearable Urges* (1999).

Kirsch is on much firmer ground when he discusses Michael Chabon's *The Amazing Adventures of Kavalier & Clay* (2000), Jonathan Safran Foer's *Everything is Illuminated* (2002) and Nicole Krauss's *The History of Love* (2005) as landmark novels that marked a shift in emphasis in twenty-first-century American Jewish fiction towards the Holocaust and, in later novels by Foer, Krauss and Joshua Cohen, towards Israel. However, here too he sometimes omits inconvenient details that complicate the argument he wants to make. For example, to reinforce his claim that this generation of writers insist on striking a note of "affirmation" at the end of their work, Kirsch claims that *Everything Is Illuminated* ends with "a final letter from Alex's grandfather, holding out hope that a better future awaits Alex's gen-eration: 'I would give everything for them to live without violence … They must begin again.'" He neglects to mention that this letter is a suicide note, leaving Alex heartbroken and his friendship with Jonathan irredeemably compromised. Similarly, Kirsch fails to mention Shalom Auslander, one of the most important American Jewish authors of the twenty-first century, whose *Hope: A Tragedy* (2012) is one of the funniest and most brilliant novels published in the last twenty years – because, I suspect, Auslander doesn't fit neatly into the story that Kirsch wants to tell in "After the Golden Age".

David Brauner is Professor of Contemporary Literature at the University of Reading (UK). He is co-editor of The Edinburgh Companion to Modern Jewish Fiction *and the author of four books:* Post-War Jewish Fiction; Philip Roth; Contemporary American Fiction *and* Howard Jacobson.

Adam Kirsch responds

I'm grateful to Professors Brauner and Cammy for their responses to my essay.
They are correct, of course, that there are plenty of Jewish writers and books that
I was unable to discuss, even in the generous space given to me by JQ. I could
quibble with some of the points Brauner raises: the suicide of Alex's grandfather
in *Everything Is Illuminated*, for instance, comes after he has been exposed as
complicit in the death of a Jewish friend in the Holocaust, and suggests that the
wicked past must be wiped away to make possible a new beginning for Alex and
Jonathan's generation. That's why his last letter ends with a declaration that he is
"complete with happiness". But I'm happy to have his reminder of writers like
Shalom Auslander and Rebecca Goldstein, who are certainly worth reading.

As for Cammy's desire to "interrogate" the "overwhelmingly male" and
"Ashkenormative" canon of American Jewish literature, it doesn't surprise me –
as Heinrich Heine said about God and forgiveness, "*C'est son métier.*" But
I think that the writers I discussed in my essay, both from the twentieth century
and the twenty-first, remain indispensable for understanding American Jewish
literature, if only because so many other writers have read and reacted to them.

Adam Kirsch is a poet and critic whose books include The People and the Books:
Eighteen Classics of Jewish Literature *and* The Blessing and the Curse:
The Jewish People and Their Books in the Twentieth Century.

Past issues

"For a long time now, the authority of knowledge has been under siege from those who march under the banner of pure belief."
—Simon Schama

The Return of History: New Populism, Old Hatreds investigates rising global populism, and the forces propelling modern nativism and xenophobia.

"Traditional principles and allegiances have given way to realpolitik." —Lina Khatib

The New Middle East: Shifting Allies, Enemies and Loyalties examines the dramatic changes unfolding in the region as new rivalries, blocs and partnerships are formed – based not on ideology but on pragmatism.

"The left has become the ideology that dare not speak its name." —Anshel Pfeffer

In *The Strange Death and Curious Rebirth of the Israeli Left*, Anshel Pfeffer takes the pulse of Israel's left wing, examining its health and prospects and dissecting the country's complex post-Netanyahu political reality.

Past issues

"If ink on paper can reassemble a world ..."
—Rachel Kadish

The Jewish world of pre-war Europe was almost destroyed. If we hold up a lantern to that darkness, what can we discover about what was lost, what survived and what could have been?

"Younger writers were freed to think about specifically Jewish questions. [Their] work has a narrower appeal. Only time will tell if it is also a deeper one." —Adam Kirsch

After the Golden Age examines the current generation of leading American Jewish writers as they grapple with questions about religion, Israel, politics and multiculturalism.

Add these past issues to your subscription when buying online.

Printed by Libri Plureos GmbH in Hamburg, Germany